Your Towns and Cities in the Great War

Crewe
in the Great War

Your Towns and Cities in the Great War

Crewe
in the Great War

Peter Ollerhead

Pen & Sword
MILITARY

For Ruth and Jonathan

First published in Great Britain in 2014 by
PEN & SWORD MILITARY
an imprint of
Pen and Sword Books Ltd
47 Church Street
Barnsley
South Yorkshire S70 2AS

Copyright © Peter Ollerhead, 2014

ISBN 978 1 78346 341 1

The right of Peter Ollerhead to be identified as the author of this work has been asserted by him in accordance with the Copyright, Designs and Patents Act 1988.

A CIP record for this book is available from the British Library.

All rights reserved. No part of this book may be reproduced or transmitted in any form or by any means, electronic or mechanical including photocopying, recording or by any information storage and retrieval system, without permission from the Publisher in writing.

Printed and bound in England
by CPI Group (UK) Ltd, Croydon, CR0 4YY

Typeset in Times New Roman

Pen & Sword Books Ltd incorporates the imprints of
Pen & Sword Archaeology, Atlas, Aviation, Battleground, Discovery,
Family History, History, Maritime, Military, Naval, Politics, Railways,
Select, Social History, Transport, True Crime, and Claymore Press,
Frontline Books, Leo Cooper, Praetorian Press, Remember When,
Seaforth Publishing and Wharncliffe.
For a complete list of Pen and Sword titles please contact
Pen and Sword Books Limited
47 Church Street, Barnsley, South Yorkshire, S70 2AS, England
E-mail: enquiries@pen-and-sword.co.uk
Website: **www.pen-and-sword.co.uk**

Contents

Acknowledgements 6
Prologue 7

Chapter 1 1914 Eager for the Fight 8
Chapter 2 1915 Crushing the Spirit of Militarism 23
Chapter 3 1916 Fighting for Freedom 39
Chapter 4 1917 Another Year of Sacrifice 53
Chapter 5 1918 Enduring to Victory 67
Chapter 6 1919 Returning to Normal? 81

Bibliography and Sources 93
Index 94

About 150 women were employed on wartime 6 inch shell production in the shell manufacturing plant at the Crewe LNWR Works.

Acknowledgements

I am only too thankful that I was born in 1937 and not fifty years earlier in 1887 or else I would have been one of that generation who endured the horrors of the Somme, Passchendaele or one of the other infamous battlefields. I stand in awe and respect at their courage and suffering. Consequently, I thank publishers Pen & Sword for giving me the privilege of recording a few details about the town and people of Crewe during the four years of conflict known then as the Great War. I am especially grateful to Nigel Cave, my editor at Pen & Sword.

The list of local persons to whom I owe a debt of gratitude for their encouragement and help over the years is too long to mention. Some, however, owing to their specific help with this book, must be named; so here they are in no particular order: Harry Jones, Jack Ollerhead, Diane Dyer, Paul Blurton, Brian Kennedy, Andrew Turner, Sylvia Smallwood and Tony Flood, who read the final draft, though all remaining errors are mine and mine alone.

For permission to use photographs or original art work I thank Mary and Colin Maclean; Dorothy Flude; Mick Kelly; Fred Ikin; Darron Back; Adrian Smith; The LNWR Society. The rest are from my own collection.

I gladly acknowledge the assistance offered, mainly on-line, from my local history colleague, Susan Chambers, who, while working on a similar book, was always ready to discuss and help with my queries and problems.

Cheshire East reference library staff at Crewe (especially Mrs Katherine Bate) have been generous with their time displaying cheerfulness and efficiency whenever I made a request for help.

Finally I must thank my wife, Rose, for her devotion and encouragement and my son and daughter, to whom this book is dedicated, for their tolerance and patience when they were young while I selfishly pursued my historical interests.

Prologue

'Where is Crewe? I said to the guardian of the iron-gate. Cross the bridge, go straight on and turn to the right, was the concise reply. So I crossed the bridge ... I arrived in Crewe' 'A day at Crewe Chambers' *Edinburgh Journal*' 1850 page 91.

CREWE ON THE eve of the Great War was seventy years old, having been planted in the rural acres of Cheshire by the Grand Junction Railway Company in March, 1843. Consequently, it differed from the nearby ancient town of Nantwich, being radical in politics and completely industrial, with a wealth of metal working trades employed on locomotive manufacture and repair. By 1846, it was controlled by the recently formed London and North Western Railway Company (LNWR), which greatly expanded the productive capacity of its workshops. Some idea of the rapid expansion of the embryonic town, into a thriving community, can be gauged by reference to population growth. In sixty years it rose from 4,571 in 1851 to 46, 497, a transformation that dominated the economy of the region.

Indicative of the town's independence was the plethora of religious denominations, many of which had never appeared previously in the region. As people migrated from all over the UK to work for the LNWR they brought the seeds of their religious beliefs with them. Unions organized by the skilled workers, is also indicative of the sturdy independence of this working class town. The need for food and other material goods meant a Co-operative Movement was founded in Crewe, less than a year after the Rochdale pioneers began trading in Lancashire and long before a similar commercial commitment was undertaken by the people of Nantwich. By 1913 Crewe Co-operative Society had over twenty branches stretching out into the surrounding villages such as Willaston, Haslington and Shavington. So successful was the Crewe Co-op that in 1896 it absorbed the Nantwich Industrial Co-operative Society twenty years after its formation.

A one industry town meant that relations between the local officials of the LNWR and the civic leaders could lead to tension as interests were threatened. Water, gas and even education were largely under the control of the railway, though from 1860 a Local Board of Health challenged the paternalism of the railway company. In 1877 local control was further strengthened when Crewe was incorporated into a municipal borough, with a council and a mayor. By 1914 the problems that concerned the civic leaders were the perpetual ones of water, sewage disposal, and the need for houses. Water remained under the control of the railway company until early in the Second World War, when Corporation water began to flow to the town.

What Crewe did possess when war was declared in 1914 was a military tradition, which dated back to at least 1864, when it was agreed at a public meeting to form what eventually became known as the 36th Cheshire Rifle Volunteers. This gave way in 1887 to the 2nd Cheshire Royal Engineer (Railway) Volunteer Corps, established with six companies. Some of the men who enrolled into the Corps served in the South African war with the Boers where twenty-six of them died. Thus it was, when the call to arms came, in 1914, there was ready response from the young men whole heartedly supported, as we shall see, by the rest of the residents of Crewe.

Chapter One

1914 Eager for the Fight

'The men are more eager today to see active service than they were fifteen years ago…' *Crewe Chronicle* 8 August 1914

IT SEEMS IMPOSSIBLE for us, living in our time of instantaneous news reporting, to realise that hardly anyone in Crewe, in late July 1914, seemed to be aware that a European war was about to engulf the continent. The *Crewe Guardian*'s main leading article, in that last week, was concerned with King George's intervention in the Irish Home Rule crisis, a deadlock which had exercised the minds of most thinking people in the town for some months. Why the possibility of a continental conflict had been ignored is strange, for the simmering tension between Austro-Hungary, Serbia and other Balkan countries had been evident for a number of years. In 1908 the Young Turks Party had carried through an armed revolution against Sultan Abdul Hamid, compelling him to grant Turkey a constitution, upsetting both Russia and Austro-Hungary. Trouble in Bulgaria, Bosnia and Herzegovina quickly followed. Without going into detail, suffice it to say that Great Britain, Serbia, Greece and Germany, also became involved in quarrels that were eventually papered over without being really resolved.

At about the same time, the Admiralty appreciated that it risked losing naval supremacy over Germany, which resulted in a squabble in the cabinet instigated by the Chancellor, Lloyd George, who wanted less money spent on Dreadnoughts and more on social reform. The agitation that followed led to a demand for more battleships with the popular cry of 'We want eight and we won't wait'. Further stirring of the diplomatic pot was caused when a German gunboat was dispatched to Agadir in Morocco in the midsummer of 1911, thereby upsetting France, the dominant Colonial power in the area. Despite much international invective that almost led to war, this third crisis in three years was resolved without recourse to armed conflict. Relations between these various European powers niggled along with occasional outbreaks of violence that all served to interfere with the seemingly vital interests of the Great Powers, namely Russia, Germany, France, Italy and Austro-Hungary. Thus it was that in 1914 the continent was a seething pit with Germany anxious to deal once and for all with its old enemy, France. Russia was looking suspiciously at an Austro-Hungary that was seeking to extend its domination over the Balkan States, while many in France still could not accept, or overlook, the shame of Germany's victory in 1871 when she lost Alsace and Lorraine.

Great Britain, despite unparalleled prosperity and a world-wide empire, viewed with distaste Germany's zeal for shipbuilding, militarism and its urgent search for colonies. With the gunshots in Sarajevo, in June 1914, killing the Crown Prince of the Austro-Hungarian Empire, the tinder of war was lit, as Germany sided with Austria, while France allied herself with Serbia. When Germany, after declaring war on France, invaded

THE POWERS AT GRIPS.

Britain Declares War on Germany.

NAVAL RESERVES CALLED OUT.

Embodiment of Territorials.

GERMANS DELIVER TWO ATTACKS ON LIEGE.

BOTH REPULSED,

Loss of 8,000 Men and Seven Guns.

Headlines from the *Crewe Chronicle* showing how the paper reported that the country was at war.

Belgium, Great Britain had hardly any option other than to join with Russia and France against the Central Powers, as Germany and her allies became known.

Meanwhile, the local papers that circulated around Crewe were not concerned with the deepening international crisis during the weeks immediately before the declaration of war. A *Crewe Guardian* report of Canon Rawnsley's sermon, on the 'Decay of Family Life', occupied far more column inches than the twenty-eight lines the paper devoted to 'the more hopeful news' regarding the Austro-Serbian dispute. Strange though it might seem, only four days before the reserves were mobilized, the editor of the local paper was commenting on the holiday season and the health of the town's children. The main military matter brought before the populace of Crewe was the resumption of the 1st Cheshires musketry training that had been interrupted by the Home Rule crisis in Ireland.

Between 31 July–4 August, 1914 the whole subject matter of both the *Crewe Guardian* and the *Crewe Chronicle* was drastically altered. Instead of being concerned with Jack Platt, the Crewe comedian, obtaining a week's booking at Llandudno; or Wilding's new shop in Blackpool, the agenda now was WAR. A leader in the *Crewe Guardian* firmly supported the government's action, citing two reasons for its approval, namely, 'duty to our friends' and the 'instinct for self-preservation'. It encouraged its

This map indicates the line of conflict on the Western Front in the summer of 1915 and which changed very little until the spring of 1918.

readers by telling them that though war meant sacrifice, 'we would face it with calmness, confidence and unflinching courage'. Neither the editor, nor his readers, could guess how much courage would be needed over the next four years by the young men of the fighting nations.

In one of his regular sermons the Rector of Coppenhall, the Reverend Cawley Reid, encouraged the volunteers for war with the words:

> 'Therefore believing the cause of our beloved King and Country is a good and true one .... we go forth with a clear conscience as a united nation and commit our cause with calmness and confidence into the hands of that Lord of hosts and God of armies who judgeth righteously.'

His was not a lone voice in the town, as all the other mainstream churches were also emphasizing the justice of the cause and appealing for volunteers. No doubt there were many other reverend gentlemen in Germany, Austria, France and Russia who were preaching the same message.

Eardley's *Crewe Almanack*, which records the momentous event of 4 August with a laconic sentence, 'War declared by Great Britain on Germany', does not mention the almost carnival-like atmosphere that pervaded the town in the first heady days of August. Most shops, especially those trading in provisions, were open late into the night, while the main Post Office did not close at all. People thronged around the offices of the *Crewe Guardian*, *Crewe Chronicle* and the *Crewe Observer*, seeking the latest information. Others gathered at the railway station, in patriotic fervour, watching until the early hours of the morning, as trains packed with troops passed through taking reservists to their depots. Regular rail traffic was not suspended despite forty or fifty crowded troop trains a day passing through. As an interesting report in *The Times* of 6 January 1915 made clear, Crewe was at the heart of the British railway system,

From contemporary accounts, there is little doubt that the war was popular with the majority of the men and women of Crewe. There were, however, a few muted protests against the outbreak of hostilities, such as the resolution passed by the local branch of the National Union of Railwaymen stating its lack of sympathy with the government's actions. The local branch of the Independent Labour Party also displayed a lack of enthusiasm that was not reflected by the average working man in Crewe.

Despite the general enthusiasm, not many hours passed before the effects of the war were noticed by

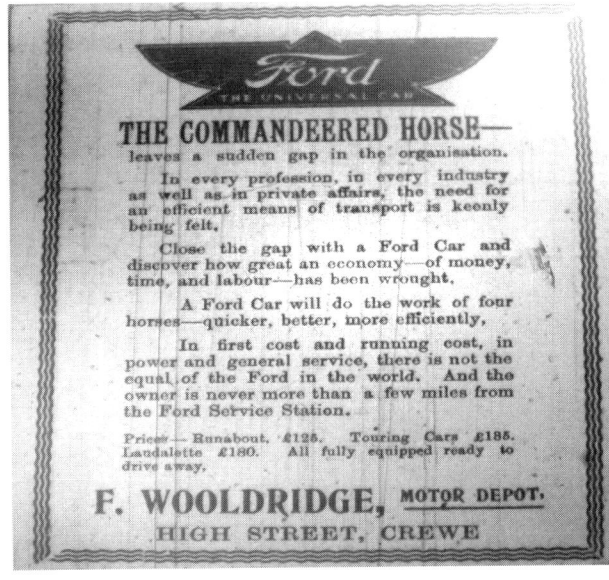

Within two weeks of the declaration of war a local car dealer stepped into the void created by the commandeering of horses to sell more cars.

Looking west in 1888 down what became Victoria Avenue. As can be seen, the Drill Hall and headquarters of the Railway Volunteers (Engineers) was on the corner of Stewart Street. The banner celebrated the visit of the Duke of Cambridge, Commander in Chief of the Forces who officially opened Queens Park. *(The LNWR Society)*

local people, especially those that had to do the shopping. Even before Great Britain had joined the conflict, prices of basic commodities were rising rapidly. At a Council meeting on 5 August, the Labour councillor, John Williams, complained that certain business houses had levied increases to the detriment of the ordinary working man. Part of the blame for these increases must be laid at the door of the more affluent householders in Crewe, as they sought to stockpile supplies, though John Bourne, the manager of Crewe Co-operative Society stores, claimed that 'outsiders' were also numbered amongst the panic buyers. The price of a sack of flour rose from ten shillings to thirteen shillings in a few hours, potatoes went up two shillings from 2/6 per cwt. while sugar increased by 50 per cent. Trade was so hectic that half-day closing was abandoned, so that counter assistants could restock the empty shelves. Even the Mayor felt compelled to intervene by pointing out that the chief sufferers in this wave of unrestrained buying were the poor, who could not afford the increased prices.

Obviously, the major effect upon the town was the immediate call up of the territorials and reservists, with the men of the naval reserve first to leave. Even before the general mobilization, the Villiers Russell twins of Audley Street left Crewe for a week's annual training aboard HMS *Formidable*, along with two other Crewe Works' men, Albert Kinlay and James Burnell. When the general mobilization was proclaimed, they all immediately signed on for the duration. They were little to know that they would be dead by the New Year. Another thirty-six men left the Post Office to join their regiments; three from Crewe Alexandra; ten from the local Co-operative Society; and three police constables, to mention but a few of the organizations that were short of staff owing to the declaration of war. A newly wed bride, Mrs D McLeod (née Miss Dicken, of Brooklyn Street), was soon separated from her husband, Donald, who had to leave Crewe with the Sick Berth Reserve on the evening of his wedding day. Owing to his imminent departure, they had managed to bring the marriage forward.

On Tuesday evening, 4 August, a few hours before war was declared, a large crowd gathered at the Square to witness a march through the town by the territorials, and other troops, led by the Crewe Works Band but, owing to the European crisis, this parade was postponed, leaving hundreds of disappointed would-be spectators. A parade did take

Iron Foundry, Crewe Works, where David Dodd of Rose Terrace worked until he volunteered for war service. He was killed in action in March 1918 fighting with the Cheshire Regiment in Egypt. *(The LNWR Society)*

place though, at the early hour of 7.00am on Sunday, 9 August; amongst the civic dignitaries present were William D Struthers, the Director of Education, HSK Feltham, the Town Clerk and Edward Vaughan, the Mayor, one of whose sons was already in uniform (sadly killed at the end of 1916). As this was a church parade, the artillery and territorials had to listen to a sermon from the Reverend Walter Bidlake, who told them to ' ... keep clean, straight and cheerful, for the next few months would bring danger.' He, amongst many others, thought it would all be over by Christmas. If only!

It had been hoped that the postponed march around the town would follow the church parade, only for Major Powell to insist on an immediate return, meaning the artillery walked back in the drizzle to Queens Park, where they had left the gun carriages and horses. Probably the first injury of the war to a Crewe man was received by Sergeant Alfred Jones, when his horse reared, leaving him in need of treatment at the nearby hospital. Enduring the now heavy rain, the contingent of artillery men marched, or rode, to Wellington, via Market Drayton. Many of the disappointed spectators could have watched the departure of the territorials on film at the local Empire cinema later in the week.

Lieutenant Wilmot Welch, with other officers, had been very busy commandeering

Members of West Street Baptist Tabernacle Boys' Life Brigade at their camp in Alderley Edge, in 1908. Many of these lads must have seen service in France.

horses from local farms and firms. To perform this task efficiently, they were issued with a pamphlet *Types of Horses Suitable for Army Remounts*, which contained purchase prices for different breeds. For instance, mounts for the cavalry would cost around £70, whereas for transport horses Welch was authorised to offer £35 to £40. Crewe Co-op suffered the loss of three of their animals to war service, as did the Ward Brothers, who ran the local horse-bus service. Some small businesses lost their solitary animal to the military. Even the local hunt had to forfeit a large proportion of its stock. Within four days of this search for horses for the Crewe Battery of the Cheshire Brigade of the Royal Field Artillery, Welch and his colleagues had obtained 290 of the 300 horses that they needed.

A recruiting office, opened at the Market Square, enrolled between 200 and 250 men during the first day. Amongst these were many members of Ezra Nixon's bible class at St Barnabas Church, five of whom still lie in foreign fields. About 10 per cent of the volunteers failed to reach the required standard of health and physique when examined by Dr Ernest Bailey, of Havelock House, a much lower percentage than the national average of around 35 per cent. Bailey's house was also utilized by his wife as a War Hospital Supply Depot. To help with the recruiting drive, Morrey, the dentist, of Gatefield Street, kindly offered free, painless extractions for those rejected because of poor teeth. It is pertinent to note that Crewe's Medical Officer, in his report for 1914, stated that only about 30 per cent of the town's 6,000 school children had sound teeth.

Sergeant F. H. Oldham, of the Crewe Division of the St John's Ambulance Brigade, asked for volunteers in answer to a telegram he had received, requesting men for the medical and ambulance services. The response was immediate, with men leaving the town next day for the Royal Navy Sick Berth Reserve and the Royal Army Medical Corps. Sergeant Oldham, having served in the Boer War, was not asking for men to do what he had not already done. It might interest some to know that Oldham's father had been the investigating officer in one of the town's most infamous murders, in January 1890.

Crewe had a connection with the cruiser *Amphion*, the first Royal Navy vessel to be sunk in the war at sea. This happened in the early morning of 6 August, when the *Amphion*, which had only been commissioned about eighteen months previously, struck a mine. Some 150 sailors and one German prisoner of war were killed in the disaster. The Crewe connection was R. Harrop, who had joined the *Amphion* when it was commissioned. Fortunately he escaped with his life to serve another day on another ship.

Saying that Crewe was a working-class town, dominated by the manufacture of locomotives, it is surprising to note the spread and variety of regiments with which the men had been associated before hostilities began. At the end of August, the *Chronicle* proudly itemized some of the illustrious units to which the sons of the town belonged, such as the Grenadier Guards, Scots Guards, 14th Hussars, 2nd and 3rd Dragoon Guards, 21st Lancers, Royal Welsh Fusiliers, South Wales Borderers and the Royal Horse Artillery.

One month into the war, the tide of volunteers was flowing unabated. Kitchener's famous appeal, especially the poster with 'Your Country Needs You' emblazoned on it, was widely published in September. Apparently, the most favoured regiments requested by the Crewe recruits were the Guards, the Lancers or the cavalry. Needless to say, most of them were disappointed and were enlisted mainly as soldiers of the Cheshire Regiment. It was reckoned that by this time around 25 per cent of the male population of the town were in the forces. A total of about 2,500 men, of whom 2,000 had formerly worked for the London & North Western Railway (LNWR), were missing from their places of work. This must have made serious inroads into the productive capacity of the Works and Motive Power department.

All the stops were being pulled out, in the early weeks of the war, to increase the number of volunteers. Lord Kitchener, the new Secretary of State for War, was possibly one of the few in government with a real understanding that the war would last longer than a few months, and would make a great levy on the wealth and manpower of the nation. An open air recruiting drive was held, on the Square, by the great and the good of the town, including councillors and clergy, who walked in procession from the Municipal Offices, in Earle Street, to the Square. Ernest Craig, the town's Tory MP, was the main speaker and urged the young men to enrol immediately. Councillor John Williams added his voice, claiming that the German Emperor was 'a damnable cad'. Joseph Stubbs, of the Crewe Music Warehouse, and choir master of the Crewe Apollo Male Voice Choir, led the martial and patriotic music. It was quite handy that the recruiting office was nearby as there were many that responded to the invitation to sign on. The only difficulty, according to contemporary evidence, was that the process of actually enlisting was long and tedious.

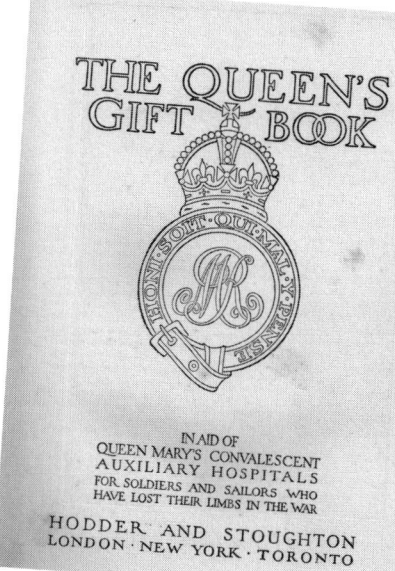

The Queen's Gift Book was one of many books published during the Great War with the sole aim of raising money for war charities.

One of the implications of this rush of recruits was the sudden decline in the income of the dependants. By the end of September soldiers' wives were granted fifteen shillings a week if they had one child, with extra for every child up to a maximum of four. In addition, a married soldier could have six pence stopped out of his pay as an allowance for his wife. An allowance would also go to a widow with a son in the services. Nationally, the London & North Western Railway Company paid two thirds of their weekly wage (up to a maximum of 10/-) to all married employees called up to serve in the armed forces, as did the Crewe Stationery Company. As Cheshire County Council also paid the same percentage of two thirds salary to the families of enlisted men, Crewe Town Council followed their example. Instantaneous with the recruiting drive, many organizations were formed to assist with any hardship. On 10 August, the Town Council's general purposes committee were discussing a telegram, from the Prince of Wales, about opening a subscription list for his recently established Relief Fund. The LNWR Chief Mechanical Engineer, C.J. Bowen Cooke acted as treasurer for all money raised in the Works. By the end of November, £3,280 had been sent from Crewe to the national treasurer.

Many and varied were the other local voluntary organizations called into existence by the first month of the war. Mrs W. Warneford, the wife of the LNWR Crewe locomotive works manager, along with other local ladies, set to work to provide hospital facilities. The Local Government Board had issued instructions for the Council to commence a 'Distress Committee', which they did before the end of August, appointing over fifty members in the process. Lady Cotton-Jodrell, wife of a Cheshire landowner, recommenced the Crewe & Nantwich Branch of the Soldiers' and Sailors' Families Association, which raised £815 by May 1915, and had assisted 189 wives, 455 children and 120 widowed mothers of reservists. Members of Crewe Primrose League were hard at work making socks, shirts and other garments. Similar activities, generated by the war, at this juncture included the League of Friendliness, Dale Tobacco Fund, a Fund for Belgian Refugees and the RSPCA Fund for Sick and Wounded Horses.

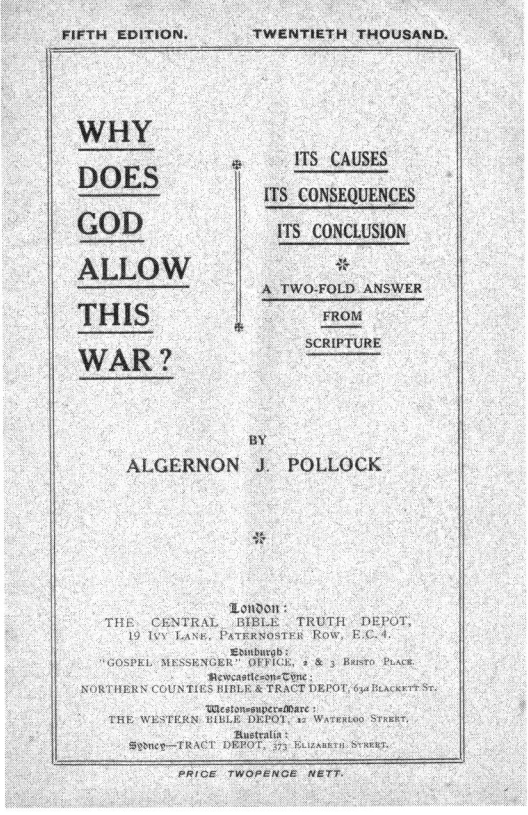

Some theologians and Christian preachers sought to explain divine intentions behind the war. A. J. Pollock occasionally preached in Crewe between 1910 and 1940.

There were subdued mutterings locally that Nantwich and the nearby rural areas were not supplying their fair share of recruits. Though the complaints might have been exaggerated, there is evidence that the response to Lord Kitchener's appeal was somewhat sluggish. Sir Wyndham Hamer, at a meeting in Whitchurch, appealed for more fighting men from the agricultural areas. He impressed upon the farmers that as a class they would be expected to contribute to the nation's fighting strength. Another speaker, Major Godsal, pleaded in bald terms to the patriotism of the farmers. According to the *Chronicle* report, '…the gathering received the suggestions in freezing silence'. The farmers countered the recruiting appeal by claiming that their sons were needed at home to do the milking. In the same edition of the *Chronicle*, Ernest Craig, Member of Parliament for Crewe, refused to appeal for more volunteers as the town had done its share.

Both the *Crewe Chronicle* and the *Crewe Guardian* sought to appease the appetite of their readers for news of the war situation, though the reality was soon made clear. The retreat from Mons and the Battle of the Marne claimed two Crewe men, Private George Morris, on 24 August, and Private Charles Alfred King, aged 29, of Lockett Street, on 10 September. He (King) was the third Crewe casualty of the war, leaving a widow and a baby of four months to mourn his death. A few days before, Private G. Davenport, another Crewe man, had been injured during the retreat from Mons. Towards the end of September, while at anchor in Zanzibar harbour, HMS *Pegasus* was attacked and sunk by the German light cruiser SMS *Konigsberg*. Amongst the thirty-eight sailors killed was James Gill, of Dewes Street, who had formerly worked in the brass foundry in Crewe Works. Other battles of 1914 including the Aisne, La Bassée and the First Battle of Ypres, in which Sergeant A.G. Hayes (Lincoln Street), Private A. Paul (Derby Street), Private S. Hilditch (Moss Square) and Private H. Manley (Naylor Street) were all killed. These men are but a representative sample of the local men who paid the ultimate price in the first months of the war.

Two months into the conflict the local papers began printing letters from soldiers at the front describing conditions. The two below give some impressions of soldiers from the town. Private J. Williams, of the Scots Greys, in a letter home to his wife wrote:

'I hope to be home at Christmas if it is all over by then. Our regiment has been doing some good work …. The French girls are not very good looking but they will give you apples and grapes and peaches by the hundred. I have not had any beer since I left England as it is not worth drinking at all. It is all wine and spirits here.'

A somewhat different view is given by Private Lockett, writing to his mother in Wistaston Road:

'Death does not trouble us much here as we see lots of them and the wounded. They are passing every minute with something blown away from them. Shells dropping around us day and night. We don't take much notice of them now …. Shells are poured out from the guns in thousands every day …. Men who were in South Africa say it was only a game of Boy Scouts to this.'

Another letter describes how a 'Jack Johnson' shell exploded amongst their battery, causing twenty-six casualties. As men were attending to the injured another shell burst sliced the farrier's head off.

It has been said that the first casualty of war is truth, a state of affairs which accounts for the many rumours that circulated the town before Christmas

Private Charles Warham was the first Crewe man to die in the Great War, though not from war wounds. His grave is in Bordon Military Cemetery, Hampshire. *(Darron Back)*

1914. One of these that caused widespread dismay, reported in the *Chronicle* of 22 August, was that a Crewe man had been killed. Sadly, this was true, though caused by disease and not through armed conflict, as Sapper Charles Warham (Charles Street), the first Crewe fatality, died in a Hampshire hospital on 15 August. The same edition (22 August), also scotched a rumour that the men in the Crewe Artillery contingent were being ill-treated and poorly fed. Towards the end of 1914, however, the editor of the *Chronicle* complained in a leading article that, '…. catering for recruits was poor as the food was poorly prepared and poorly served.' A few hours of hysterical panic ensued in the last days of August, when a German spy was supposed to be loitering in the Earle Street area. A train full of Russian troops was reported as passing through Crewe, though no mention was made of snow on their boots, as was the case in other towns when the same gossip was whispered abroad. One of the grisliest rumours must have been that the Kaiser was boiling little children for the war effort. Such suggestions could only take root in the giddy atmosphere of 1914.

One of Conrad Reiss's shops was among those vandalised in the anti-German riots of October 1914, when any Crewe business with a German sounding name was in danger from what was often a drink fuelled mob.

Silly tales, similar to the one just quoted about the Kaiser, were eagerly accepted, mainly through the anti-German hysteria that swept the country resulting in Prince Louis Battenberg, the First Sea Lord, resigning in October 1914. King George V held out longer before he, too, changed the family's surname from Saxe-Coburg and Gotha to Windsor. In a similar action, the LNWR altered the name of a couple of their locomotives from Germanic to Belgic and from Teutonic to Czar.

Mindless pseudo-patriotism led to riots in the town on the night of 24 October, when a crowd of several thousands gathered outside John Gronbach's butcher's shop in Victoria Street. Cries of 'Shift the Germans', along with similar inflammatory shouts, were made by the ringleaders at the front of the mêlée. When the police told them to move on they refused, demanding loudly for the Germans to be brought out, as they did not want Germans in Crewe. Suddenly, amidst the abusive cries, stones were hurled at the shop so violently that the windows were broken, stimulating the perpetrators to enter the premises, where they proceeded to empty the shelves and cupboards of meat and associated food.

Most of those that were eventually charged with the affray were at the time under the influence of alcohol, so therefore took little notice of the authorities. Even though fourteen constables surrounded the shop and allowing Dr Wilson, of Delamere Street, to plead with the crowd to disperse, it was all to no avail. Joseph Stockton, along with Norman Dale, accompanied by a large group of delinquents, then further incited the crowd by inviting them to walk to Conrad Reiss's pork butcher's shop in Mill Street. This they did, where again the premises were broken into, ransacked and robbed, though fortunately the Presbyterian pastor, the Reverend R.W. Roberts, bravely sheltered the Reiss family in his manse.

Not satisfied with the mayhem they had created at the two shops they had despoiled, Stockton, Dale, Thomas Worrall with other hooligans decided to attack the premises of Bort, another pork butcher, of 176 Edleston Road. By now it was 2.00 am on Sunday morning, yet still they were bent on destroying anything that they considered German. The fact that Bort had already been interned was nothing to the baying mob. Neither was the fact that Gronbach, who had been a naturalized Englishman for a decade or more, regularly donated to many local war charities. Bort's shop was illegally entered and pillaged, leaving two ladies living in the back of the premises terrified. With the lust for damage assuaged, and the effects of the alcohol wearing off, the crowd dispersed, leaving the centre of the town to resume its normal Sabbath slumber.

Another, smaller, crowd assembled on Monday evening outside John Menicken's butcher's shop in Edleston Road, at around 9.00 pm, under the delusion that such a surname was Germanic. Fortunately, the presence of the police and the appeals of C.J. Bowen Cooke, the Chief Mechanical Engineer of the LNWR, helped to disperse the crowd. Ironically, Menicken's son served on the Somme before being taken to hospital with heart trouble in 1916. About a month later, in November 1914, another smaller crowd demonstrated in front of Lees, the pork butcher of Victoria Street, accusing him of being a German. These misguided pseudo-patriots were not to know, of course, that John Lees, the son of the butcher, would die of wounds received in August 1918, while serving with Royal Welsh Fusiliers.

Another example of this anti-German craze is the 10/- fine levied against a Crewe man for making obscene remarks about a shopkeeper's supposed Germanic origin early in December 1914. Anti-German feelings were dominant in a squalid debate, in the council chamber of Crewe Corporation, where members were divided over the chairmanship of the health sub-committee. Some of the elected representatives violently disagreed with Councillor Withoff occupying the chair. The ostensible reason was that he (Withoff) was a butcher, though why that should debar him is difficult to judge. Perhaps a more potent factor is that it was claimed by an opponent, during the heated proceedings, that he had German blood running through his veins. This was true, for his grandfather had migrated to Crewe from Prussia in the middle years of the nineteenth century.

The perpetrators of the October riots were summonsed to appear at the local magistrates' court. In front of the bench the fifteen culprits were not as fired up with patriotic fervour when the twenty charges were read out. Fines of 1/6d to 10/-, with the alternative of fourteen days in prison, were imposed against the culprits, most of whom pleaded guilty. This was not the end, as restitution had to be made to the shopkeepers, who had lost out when their premises were damaged and looted. A total

An LNWR omnibus on Nantwich Road Crewe just prior to the Great War. By 1913 Crosville of Chester were also operating bus services between Crewe, Nantwich and Sandbach.

of £594 compensation was awarded to Gronbach, Reiss, Bort, James and Eames, the latter two suffering collateral damage, as they were neighbours to the butchers.

No evidence has come to light of any Crewe soldiers taking part in the famous football matches played in No Man's Land on the Western Front, during the unofficial truce over Christmas, 1914. There is, however, an interesting letter from Private Albert Jones, of the North Staffordshire Regiment, who had enlisted in 1892 and was called up as a reservist.

'In the trenches on Christmas Day we had a rather moving experience …. On Christmas Eve [the Germans] put little torch lights along the top of their trenches and commenced singing carols till late at night. They would give song then shout across to us to encore. Of course we gave one and they would cheer us. We kept it up for two or three hours till they wanted to get more friendly and met us half way. Things then went quiet until Christmas morning when we met …. shaking hands with one another as if we had known them for years. It was a clear frosty morning, the enemy's trenches only 50 or 60 yards away. We exchanged cigars and cigarettes quite freely … . The first thing they commenced to do was to pay a last tribute to their dead, which they at once buried.'

Private Jones went on to write that the Germans, who belonged to a Saxon Regiment, expressed the wish that the war would soon end. Sadly, almost another four years were to pass before it was all over.

Chapter Two

1915 Crushing the Spirit of Militarism

'It would not be sufficient to drive the Germans out of France and Belgium which they had desecrated. They would have to crush the spirit of militarism and destroy it.' Ernest Craig MP for Crewe. *Crewe Chronicle*, 13 March 1915

NOT ONLY THE war reports from France cast a gloom over the town around the first Christmas of the conflict, for the weather, too, seemed to add to the general despondency. Very heavy rain, floods, frost, snow and the thickest fog for over two decades did much to dampen what Christmas cheer there was. Apparently neither light from the electric street lamps or from the many gas lanterns that were supposed to provide illumination could penetrate the thick fog. All vehicular traffic ceased, meaning that walking was the only way around. Contemporary accounts tell of a man who found himself in Mill Street, when he was convinced he was in Market Street. Two troop trains collided in the fog at the station, breaking many carriage windows, but fortunately injuring nobody.

No sooner had the weather improved than the town was rocked by the death of four young men, who were killed when HMS *Formidable* was sunk by a German submarine

Some of Crewe's soldiers were captured at various times during the four years of war, meaning that they spent time in German prison camps suffering severely from cold and hunger until food parcels began to arrive from the UK. *(Mick Kelly)*

just off the south coast. Two of the four bodies of the young men from Crewe were washed ashore at Lyme Regis, but the other two, James Burnell and Albert Kinlay, were never found. Two recovered bodies were the Villiers Russell twins of Audley Street; a great outburst of communal mourning accompanied the funeral, which must have seemed somewhat ironic to the rest of the families in Crewe that had lost sons and husbands in the first five months of the war. It is understandable, though, that a civic funeral was arranged, as these were the first bodies that had been returned to the town. What is not so easy to grasp is why this civic emphasis upon the death of these two lads is continued to the present day, as a memorial board, dedicated to their memory, was erected about twenty years ago in the main foyer of the Municipal Buildings. Where else in the town are victims of the Great War singled out for such notice? What the many relatives who lost loved ones in that conflict would make of the Council's action in honouring just two out of the hundreds who died is not difficult to guess.

By the time the funeral of the twins was held, about fifteen other Crewe men had been killed in action, with thirty-five or so wounded and ten languishing in prison camps. Later in January, Mrs Sherwin of Alexander Street received a death notice for Gunner Sherwin, her husband, which was revoked a few days later. This was not as bad as the wife of Corporal F.A. Jones, who received notice that her husband had been killed; this was then cancelled, saying he was alive, only to receive a telegram a couple of weeks later informing her that he had been killed on the morning of the 11 February. This time it was for real.

Another lesser terror that visited the homes of the soldiers was the knowledge that a relative was a prisoner of war. Only a few weeks into the conflict, men from Crewe had been captured by the enemy, mainly at Mons, to be marched off to camps in Germany. By May 1915, this company of the captured with local connections amounted to around thirty-five men. Amongst them was Private A. Farrell, of Underwood Lane (later repatriated), who sent a card to his wife with the biblical reference 'Luke chapter fifteen and verse seventeen' appended. On referring to this verse:

'And when he came to himself, he said, How many of my father's hired servants have bread enough and to spare, and I perish with hunger,'

it was obvious to his wife that this was an urgent, yet secretive, plea for food.

Private F. Cooke, of the 2nd Cheshires, was not so subtle with his entreaties, as his letter to his mother in Market Street states:

'I am a prisoner of war. I want you to send to me a parcel as soon as you get this letter. Make a cake and put me some cheese, butter, and biscuits in and a bar of soap and don't forget plenty of twist [tobacco]. Put them in a strong box and if you can afford it a safety razor as I have not had a shave for months. I want you to send me a parcel every week. We are only allowed to write two letters and six postcards a month.'

Another prisoner of the Germans, Private Joseph Pettigrew, of Davenport Street, was even more ravenous, for he requested a packet of tea, a bag or two of sugar, two tins of cocoa, four packets of flour, a dozen boxes of matches, a packet of salt, a pound of butter, milk, biscuits, cakes, cigarettes, 2lb of cheese, two big loaves, a box of Quaker

1915 CRUSHING THE SPIRIT OF MILITARISM   25

William and Alice Stone of Crewe with their baby daughter Florrie, undisturbed by thoughts of war, death and widowhood. *(Mick Kelly)*

Poignant message from Private William Stone, to his daughter Florrie (John Street), made even more poignant when it is realised that he was killed in action a few weeks later fighting with the Royal Welsh Fusiliers in July 1915. *(Mick Kelly)*

oats, a few shillings and two wooden pipes.

The trouble was that the prisoners at the various camps had no idea how shortages and inflation had hit the home front, where by January 1915 the purchasing power of a sovereign had dropped by 20 per cent. Freight expenses continued to increase and as mutton was imported from Australia and New Zealand, eggs from Denmark, beef from Argentina and wood from Scandinavia, costs were almost prohibitive. During an angry debate in the Council Chamber in February, Councillor Yates made the claim that rising food and commodity prices were equivalent to a 30 per cent wage cut. However the cost of living was gauged, it is obvious that buying extra food for relatives in German prison camps was not an easy task.

At a Town Council meeting, in May 1915, the Mayor reported that he had received a postcard, from Sergeant W. Barrow, asking that clothing and cigarettes be sent for twelve Crewe men who were prisoners with him in a camp in Germany. He had also sent one to the Reverend W. Bidlake, of Christ Church, with the same request. One of the organizations that took up the task of regularly supplying food parcels and cigarettes to the starving prisoners was the LNWR Employees Committee, led by C.R. Bates, who later moved to Rolls-Royce at Derby. He was influential in Rolls-Royce setting up in Crewe in 1938. By mid-summer, this committee was despatching around eighteen parcels a month to the Crewe prisoners, each one containing bread, butter, tea, sugar, milk, cocoa, sardines, syrup, Oxo cubes and cigarettes. What is perhaps surprising is that they were usually intact when they reached their destination in Germany.

Another voluntary local organization that also joined in this supply of sustenance was the Crewe League of Friendliness, which was formed only two months into the war.

Sergeant W Barrow of Crewe sent a letter to the Mayor requesting clothing and cigarettes for himself and other prisoners from the town. In the post-war years he married the widow of Private W Stone. *(Mick Kelly)*

The Reverend Joseph Pickthall, pastor of Hightown Congregational Church, held a meeting in the Mechanics' Institution for people who were interested in 'helping the homes where the menfolk have left for the front also to sit and sew for soldier's needs'. So immense was the challenge to care adequately for the families of the enlisted men that the League divided its charges into at least four sections with about five hundred women in each section. An example of this would be in August 1915, when the wives and mothers of 'B' section should have been entertained to tea in the grounds of The Brooklands; because of inclement weather they had to resort to St Paul's Schoolroom, whereas the 'A' section repaired to the Congregational Schoolroom.

Catering for tea parties was not a simple matter, as prices continued to rise with commodities getting scarcer by the day. A major factor in the rise of the cost of living was the continuing increase in freight rates, which rose from twelve shillings and six pence a ton to eighty nine shillings a ton in a matter of three months. The local paper also joined in these complaints of profiteering, with a phrase that would not be acceptable today: 'Even the shipper is exacting profits with a Jew's hand.' Other bodies were more sympathetic to the complexities of the times, with the Roman Catholic Cardinal Bourne relaxing the dietary regulations about meat and fish on Fridays. The purchasing power of a pound continued to fall; meaning that the only solution to the cost of living crisis was the commencement of regular wage rises, under the masquerade of a war bonus.

As costs increased the rate of recruiting decreased, and though the two were not linked, there were complaints in some quarters of able-bodied men leaving agriculture and other low paid jobs, for posts in munitions factories. This led to demands for compulsory military service, with the first of these occurring in a Council meeting, in April 1915, when Alderman J.H. Kettell stated it would be a good thing, whereas the veteran Liberal and ex-Vice-President of the Primitive Methodist Conference, Alderman William McNeill, did not. Two months later it was being aired again in the same forum,

Until August 1914, when he enlisted into the 11th Cheshires, Thomas Henry Palin, of Naylor Street, worked in the LNWR Joiners' Shop (shown above). In September 1915 the 11th Battalion sailed for France, where Private Palin was killed by a shell fragment after only three months at the Front. *(The LNWR Society)*

when Councillor Bullock, the photographer of High Street, introduced a resolution demanding compulsory military service '… not as a Conservative but as an Englishman'. His son Charles would be killed in action two months before the war's end.

Abraham Jervis reported to his fellow councillors that there were cases of men earning three pounds a week with sons eligible for enlistment, but they thought more of the money than of their duty to the country. He went on to say that he hoped that action would be taken to bring '… the slackers to a sense of duty and to get them to the front'. It ought to be noted that his two sons had enlisted a fortnight previous to the debate. When the resolution was put to the vote it was passed sixteen votes to seven, with the octogenarian William McNeill and other Liberals, still opposed to compulsion. Copies of this resolution were sent to Prime Minister Herbert Asquith, the Leader of the Opposition and Earl Kitchener.

While Earl Kitchener was Secretary of State for War the voluntary principle of

A meeting in the LNWR Works in 1915, which passed the resolution, 'We, the working men of Crewe, will do all that is humanly possible to increase the output of munitions, and stand by our comrades in the trenches.'

recruiting was maintained, though it was increasingly being challenged, as was his position as Secretary of State. Another resolution was passed by the whole Town Council, in June 1915, expressing 'its unabated confidence in Lord Kitchener and at the same time [desires to] express its indignation at the unjustifiable and personal attacks of a certain section of the Press'. These expressions of loyalty were also sent off to the appropriate authority. Further support was provided locally when the Council agreed, at the behest of a parliamentary committee, to display extra-large recruiting posters on various hoardings throughout the town.

Appeals to patriotism went on apace, with regular meetings and rallies being arranged at suitable places in the town. Two examples, within a month of each other, were those held on Crewe Market Square and in the LNWR Works. The one on the Square, which asked for more volunteers, had the mayor in attendance, along with a contingent from the Cheshire Regiment, including the regimental band, the Town Clerk, HSK Feltham, Joseph Davies, prospective MP for Crewe and Councillor J. Williams, an eager recruiter from the Labour Party. The main speakers were Captain Finlow and Captain E.G. Hodgkison. This latter was previously a teacher at the Secondary School in Ruskin Road,

a profession he would take up again when hostilities ceased. He is reported as saying that he had been on holiday in France in August 1914 and:

> 'the first thing I did when I returned was to get permission to go and enlist as a private. I would rather be wounded over there than be a slacker over here. There are lots of young men left in Crewe behind a counter doing girl's work who ought to be out fighting.'

Hodge, or 'Bodge', as he was known to his students in later years, must have hit a chord, as over one hundred men volunteered on that occasion.

About a month later a series of rallies were held in the LNWR Works, which were definitely not for recruiting purposes, as strident appeals were made to increase industrial production. The background for this was the so-called 'shells scandal', whipped up by the *Daily Mail* which claimed that the Battle of Neuve Chapelle was not successful, owing to a shortage of artillery shells. This eventually resulted in the formation of a coalition government and the appointment of Lloyd George as Minister of Munitions, in May 1915. Crowds numbering between 1,200 and 1,400 people assembled within the Works to listen to Bowen Cooke, the Chief Mechanical Engineer, or Ernest Craig, MP for Crewe. Needless to say John Williams, the Labour councillor, added his support to the pleas for increased production. One of the planks of Craig's speech was a request, from Lloyd George, for all trade union rules and regulations to be relaxed, so that unskilled men (or women) could work alongside skilled with no demarcation disputes, promising that all privileges would be restored after the war. The assembled men, for their part, pledged that they would do all in their power to increase the output of

Private John Nevitt's memorial card from 1915, when he was killed in action, aged 23, at Gallipoli. His grave is in Azmak Cemetery, Sulva, on the coast of the Aegean Sea, Turkey, a long way from Havelock Street, Crewe, where he was born. *(Mary and Colin Maclean)*

munitions and to stand by their colleagues in the trenches.

Mid-summer, 1915, saw the National Registration Act passed, which could be considered a halfway house to shelter those who demanded compulsory enlistment. At least, that is what one Crewe councillor considered the Act implied:

> 'The registration at Crewe will probably disclose a fairly large number of young men who are still available for military service.'

To facilitate the requirements of this Act, all Crewe schools were closed for a fortnight to allow forty teachers to visit about nine thousand households to collect data. A further move towards compulsion occurred when Prime Minister Asquith invited Lord Derby, as the newly installed Director of Recruiting, to introduce a scheme in October, whereby men between 18 and 40 attested their agreement to serve when called upon.

According to the *Crewe Chronicle*, about another six hundred Crewe men had joined the colours under the Derby scheme. Amongst these was Reginald Berks, of Buxton Avenue, killed in action on 10 July 1917, aged 28. He was accepted for the Royal Warwickshire Regiment while working in Birmingham, though he had previously tried many times to enlist, only to be rejected. A young coppersmith, John R. Rimmer (Oak Street), enlisted into the Cheshires under the same scheme. He was numbered amongst the Somme dead in July 1916.

That autumn a military tattoo was held on the Alexandra Sports Ground, in the presence of Colonel Sir Edward Cotton-Jodrell, Bowen Cooke, Joseph Davies, the Mayor and Corporation and around ten thousand of Crewe's population. In addition to these, the Volunteers (a type of Home Guard), marched behind three bands from the Square to the stadium in Earle Street. Despite the military demonstrations and many speeches, including one from Sir Edward, who reminded the men present that they would be asked in coming days 'What did you do in the Great War', not one person responded when the appeal was made for men to enlist. It was obvious that the voluntary principle had run its course, though a few more months were to pass before enlistment was made mandatory.

The Volunteers mentioned above were formed at the beginning of March to help

Hill 60, Belgium (2002), which is where Private Albert Harrison aged 18 of Martin Street, was killed on 6 May 1915 while fighting with the 1st Cheshires.

protect the country in the wake of an invasion by the Germans. The prime mover locally in this organization was Major J.N. Jackson, the LNWR's chief draughtsman at Crewe, who lived in Wellington Square. He, along with Ernest Craig M.P. and Bowen Cooke of the LNWR, arranged a meeting in the Town Hall in an attempt to persuade the older men of the town to enlist. The unfortunate fact that the room was half empty did not stop Major Jackson, an avid military man, from enthusiastically recommending the idea and becoming the officer commanding the Crewe Company. It was emphasized that, as no state money would be available, all expenses would have to be met by voluntary contributions. This, no doubt, was the reason for the make-shift uniform of a grey Norfolk jacket, breeches and puttees which, along with regular parades, marches and military exercises in the Drill Hall, satisfied the urge to be considered part of the struggle.

Whereas Major Jackson had initially envisaged a membership of about 400, only sixty Crewe men had enrolled by the late spring of 1915, by which date the erstwhile leader had extended his command by including twenty-one men from Alsager, seventy from Nantwich and sixty from Sandbach. Whether it was the prospect of shooting practice at Hatherton rifle range, or being out-volunteered by Nantwich, or Jackson's complaint of apathy on the part of his townspeople, there was a late surge in enlisting, which took Crewe recruits to over a hundred by the summer. Amongst these were Abraham Jervis (builder), Fred Withoff, (butcher), Thomas Bamford, (headmaster) and William Dishart, proprietor of a private school. Despite two of these being members of the Town Council, no financial support was offered when Jackson and the other leaders asked for help. From contemporary accounts, it would seem that some local people considered the Volunteer Movement a joke, as the *Chronicle* commented in June 1915:

> 'Some look upon the movement in a spirit of levity and imagine that a number of harmless and amiable middle-aged men are playing at soldiers; [the critics] are as ill-informed as they are unimaginative.'

It must have been some consolation to the elderly recruits that they had raised sufficient funds to have been equipped with rifles before mid-summer's day. An interesting event, linked to this time but that had nothing to do with the birth of the Volunteers, was the birth of a baby to one of the Belgian refugees living in the town, who named her daughter 'Crewe'.

So many young men had volunteered, since August 1914, that a yawning gap had appeared in the workshops and commercial desks that needed filling if production was to be maintained. Females were a source of extra labour that had not yet been tapped, although there were some who were reluctant to admit that women could fill the gaps left vacant by the departure of the men. It was imperative that such a move was made. The *Chronicle*'s comment about vacancies in the LNWR General Offices sums up the prevailing attitude to employing women:

> 'There is a good deal of work in such offices which can be done nearly, if not quite as well, by girls as by men.'

That being so, over the next few months females were appointed as LNWR ticket collectors, postal workers (sorting and delivering), bus conductors, farm labourers and commercial window cleaners. In addition, the Education Committee allowed women teachers to remain in post after marriage. One of the jobs that ladies found difficulty with was driving an ambulance, as they could not carry a stretcher into the hospital. Perhaps the biggest shift of female labour was the employment of ladies on munitions in the LNWR Works. The upper storey of the locomotive stores was transformed into a workshop especially for these aspiring engineers. Only women between 18 and 21 could be engaged, with the further proviso that their father must be a LNWR employee.

One new element of war that had never troubled the UK previously was the possibility of explosive devices dropped from the air upon civilians. A Zeppelin airship first appeared over the shores of England in the last days of 1914. By the following April, London had suffered its first air raid, an action that created an outcry against 'German barbarism', while at the same time introducing a form of 'black-out' in every town. Crewe received its share of Zeppelin panic in March 1915 when a rumour was spread abroad that an airship was in the vicinity, a rumour magnified by the warning blasts from the LNWR buzzer. Winifred Lear, in her book *Down the Rabbit Hole,* records how her family, in Heathfield Avenue, dealt with the scare by sheltering under the stairs. After remembering to turn off the gas, Winifred's imagination took over:

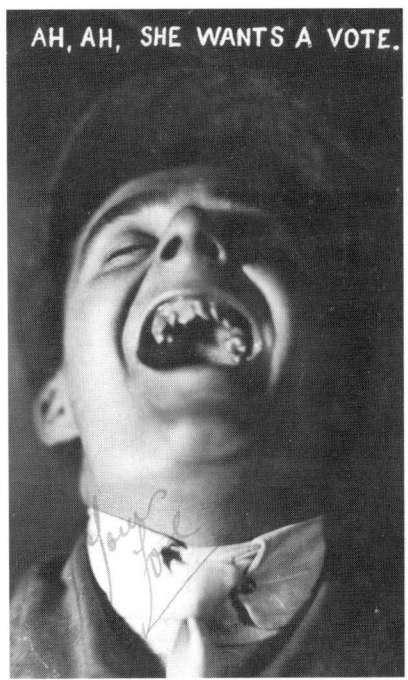

There was a prevailing attitude in Edwardian Britain amongst many men that women were incapable of rational thought and actions. The Great War created many vacancies in the labour market where, when given the chance, women proved their worth.

> 'I tried to visualize what life would be like in a house with just the stairs left standing and I could feel my enthusiasm for air-raids waning. 'Oh God,' I prayed under my breath, 'please make the Zeppelin drop its bombs on Birmingham so there won't be any left for Crewe.'

She went on to say how they all emerged unscathed from the stairs when her great aunt called to tell them it was all an unnecessary precaution, as there had been no Zeppelin near to the town.

All through 1915 the local papers listed the death tally each week, meaning that no reader could be in doubt of the awful cost of the conflict. One local man, who lost his life when HMS *Vicknor* hit a mine on 13th January and sank off the coast of Ireland, was George Lowe, formerly of Martin Street, who had moved to Birkenhead to work in Cammell Laird's shipyard. As a member of the Royal Naval Reserve, he was called up in August 1914, as were the Russell twins, though his death did not receive the publicity that theirs did.

One Crewe man, who was killed in action on land in the first days of January 1915, 18-year-old Private William Mullock, of Goddard Street, was serving with the 1st Cheshires when he fell. Three weeks later, Daniel and Lydia Holme, of Henry Street, received the news that their son, Sapper Joseph Holme, would never return to Crewe.

Amos Barrow, another local man who died of wounds in the early days of the New Year, was the first member of the Crewe Brotherhood movement to give his life for King and Country. This organization was already involved in welfare work among the families of Crewe, through its links with the League of Friendliness. Brotherhood activities, which began at the instigation of the Congregational pastor, the Reverend C. Barry, in 1911, were supposed to bridge the gap between manual workers and the church. By the end of 1914 around 10 per cent of the 1200 members of the Brotherhood had enlisted. Private Amos Barrow, of the 1st Cheshires, who had formerly worked for Crewe Co-operative Society in the grocery department, lived with his grandmother in Market Street. This 20-year-old man was wounded in the head and arms a week into the New Year, and succumbed to these injuries on the morning of the 12 January.

When the 1915 fighting season arrived with the return of spring, Crewe men were involved in its major battles. That at Neuve Chapelle in March 1915 claimed the life of a local boxer, Private Joseph Dunne of the Cameronians (Scottish Rifles), who lodged with his brother-in-law at 50 Peel Street. One month earlier, Dunne's landlord, Corporal Francis A. Jones of the Dorset Regiment, had also laid down his life. (This was the Jones whose wife had received false news of his death.) Amongst the many killed in the Second Battle of Ypres, fought in April and May, was 32-year-old Acting Sergeant Thomas Bebbington of the 1st Cheshires. Before enlisting he lived with his wife, Marcella, at 34 Sandbach Street. No doubt his mother Hannah, of Martin Street, was also deeply upset when she received the news.

Late in June a particularly vivid letter from Private H. Kirkham of the 2nd Cheshires

Mill Street Railway Hospice (opened in 1893), where it was planned that local victims of Zeppelin raids would have been treated. Fortunately, bombing never occurred in Crewe. *(The LNWR Society)*

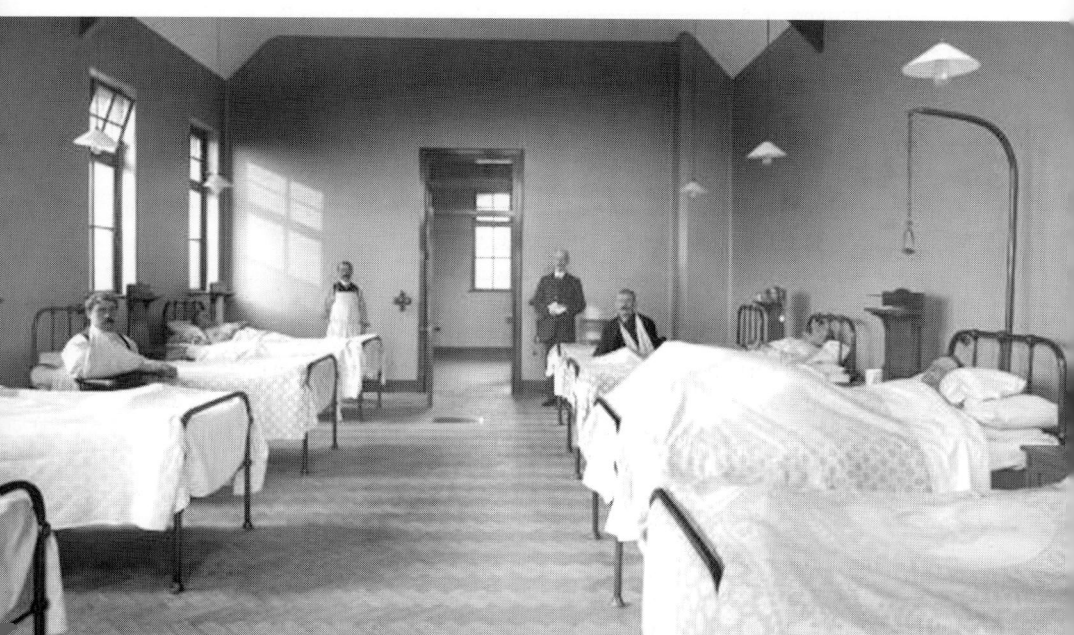

Rosina Bradley of Moss Square was buried in this grave forty-three years after her husband William, who died from shell shock in November 1916. She also suffered the loss of her son Arthur in 1916 when HMS *Defence* sank with all hands at the Battle of Jutland.

who had been in action at Bellewaerde, near Ypres, was published in the *Chronicle*:

'Shrapnel came over and burst all around us. It came down just like hail. Men went down and others could not help them … . We have dodged shells and bullets and I cannot realise how I was not hit … . A lot of us were gassed badly and many killed through its poison … . The enemy is brutal and cunning.'

Not all soldiers were killed in action, however, for Private Harry Prophett (Thomas Street) of the Cheshires died in Germany at this time, as a prisoner of war. He is buried far away from Crewe, in Niederzwehren Military Cemetery, in Kassell.

War news from France did not always cause sorrow, as often times promotions to higher rank were reported in the local press. In the *Chronicle*, of early March 1915, the parents of Walter Lightfoot were gratified to see their son had been promoted. One month later the son of Wilmot Eardley, the publisher of *Eardley's Crewe Almanack*, was commissioned as second lieutenant in the Royal Engineers. Parental pride however, must have been tempered a few weeks later, when Lieutenant Eardley fractured his skull when engaged in building a bridge at Chatham Barracks.

Decorations for bravery on the field of battle were another cause of celebration. One of the first of these was the Distinguished Service Medal (DSM) won by Gunner Peter Livingstone, a member of Beech Street Unitarian Church, whose family home was in Queen Street. He was serving on HMS *Lion*, in January 1915, at the Battle of Dogger Bank. After the ship was damaged he dived into the sea to place the emergency damage mats, saving the ship from disaster. When the news of this action and Livingstone's award filtered through to Crewe, Miss Maud Cooke of The Brooklands wrote to the

Council asking for a suitable civic response. Not satisfied with a letter of recognition from the mayor, she demanded and received a more public celebration for the young sailor. By the war's end over three hundred former local LNWR employees had earned military honours of one kind or another. It is not recorded if Miss Cooke arranged for a hero's return for any of these.

Persistent reports in the local papers of the Crewe men killed in action only increased the anti-German phobia that still pervaded the town, especially after the sinking of the *Lusitania* in May 1915. Pork butchers of Germanic origin from Cumbria and south Staffordshire regularly traded at the cattle auctions in the Gresty Road area. After appeals from many farmers and butchers, Manley's, the auctioneers, agreed not to accept bids from aliens, causing the banned butchers to return home without a purchase. A leading member of Crewe Trades Council organized a meeting on the Square demanding the internment of every alien in the country, and this despite 19,000 of them already in detention. Baroness Marie von Schroder, of The Rookery, Worleston, had to write to the *Chester Courant* to deny that her son was fighting for Germany. He was actually a captain in the 9th Lancers, while she was doing much good work in the local emergency hospitals. A relative of hers was killed in 1917, fighting for the British.

One of the Crewe men killed in action at this time has his name engraved on a family tombstone near to the crematorium in Crewe Cemetery, and also on the Menin Gate. His name was William Nicol, a private in the Liverpool Scottish, who died on 16 June fighting at Hooge, near Ypres. Attached to Nicol's battalion was Noel Chavasse, an RAMC doctor, who in a letter to his father, the Bishop of Liverpool, noted that only 130 men were able to march back on 17 June out of 550 who had marched out the previous day. This same letter gives a graphic account of this horrific, yet typical, engagement, in which Chavasse was awarded a Military Cross and Nicol died.

To commemorate the first anniversary of the declaration of war, a year during which at least fifty Crewe men had fallen on the field of battle, a rally was called on the Square in the centre of Crewe. Thousands turned out to mark the occasion, including Ernest Craig MP, the Mayor and Corporation, prominent tradesmen, the Fire Brigade in full dress uniform and a troop of Boy Scouts. They all marched in procession from the Municipal Buildings in Earle Street to the Square, where the Crewe Company of Volunteers was waiting under the command of Major J.N. Jackson and D.H. McCurtain. The Volunteers, in their make-shift uniforms, marched behind the Crewe LNWR Works Band from the Secondary School in Ruskin Road. The commemorative celebrations kicked off with the singing of *O God our Help in Ages Past*, then Bowen Cooke read a letter from Lloyd George, emphasizing the urgent necessity of munitions. The mayor began the speeches by rejoicing that the time was not far off when they would be celebrating a great victory. He told the assembled company that: 'they were bound to win and in the end their victory would be handsome.' After further tirades and lectures from Aldermen McNeill and Badger, various councillors and C.J. Bowen Cooke, the band struck up and the Volunteers paraded behind it once more and the crowd dispersed. On the way back, a Volunteer needed artificial respiration, an event that provoked the formation of an ambulance section. Despite the mayor's rejoicing that victory was not far off, the fighting continued, meaning many more tears would flow in 1915 as the names of the dead and maimed were communicated to the affected families.

Amongst the many interesting letters from soldiers sent home to Crewe, were some pathetic ones from officers and 'chums' describing the deaths of some of the sons of the town. There is not sufficient space to mention everyone, so only a few can be cited. One of the major engagements of 1915 was the ill-fated Dardenelles attack against the Turks. Captain E. Hodgkison, wrote of his experiences to the *Gridiron*, the magazine of Ruskin Road School:

> 'Where I was the Turks were about 400 yards off, but not far away they were within 80 yards. I was out on patrol three nights ... saw them at work and got back safely to report. It's awful to be in 'no man's land'... for hundreds of dead Turks and Britons lie in all stages of decay and as you crawl among them a suspicion strikes you that some of the apparent dead may be very much alive ... some of them were, as they proved by opening fire on my patrol.'

A German soldier's wartime greetings card to his family. On the reverse is a message in German to his 6-year-old daughter. When Hitler came to power the daughter moved to the UK as a Jewish refugee becoming a respected general practitioner.

Meanwhile, Sapper Fred Francis of the East Lancs Royal Engineers, whose wife lived in Fleet Street (now Meredith Street), was killed in the same campaign on 30 July. When this futile attempt to knock Turkey out of the war was drawn to a conclusion, in early 1916, Sergeant J.E. Mills (Lea Avenue) was awarded a Distinguished Conduct Medal (DCM) for gallant service during the withdrawal of his regiment. George Pottie, was at 60 one of the oldest Crewe men to be killed in action, when his ship HMS *Ramsey* was torpedoed on 8 August 1915. His father was a founder member of many early organizations in the town, such as the Co-operative Society and the Mechanics' Institution.

July saw Crewe Clarion Club appealing to the council to allow mixed bathing in the park lake only to be refused permission for a rather quaint reason. Apparently, '... neither Crewe nor Nantwich is ready for mixed bathing as a swimming bath is a place where the art of swimming is taught.' Elsewhere it was reported that one hundred and fifty-seven dogs and ninety-six cats had been destroyed in the town's lethal chamber. On a lighter note, a flower seller raising money for the hospital on Alexandra's Day sold a kiss for half a crown instead of a flower for a penny; while Crewe's Medical Officer, ever mindful of the health of the people, warned that bicycles caused heart strain in 12-year-old boys. Regarding hospitals, it was reported that the local Red Cross Hospital which had been established in Webb's Orphanage could accommodate about fifty soldiers treating them for shrapnel wounds, gas poisoning or other war injuries. At different times money was raised for war charities at concerts where local entertainers such as Lou Townley, F.V. Hanley, Miss Mavor, W. Horabin and Jack Platt took the stage.

In October 1915, towards the end of the major British offensive at Loos, another Crewe family was devastated to receive a letter from a captain in the Rifle Brigade concerning their son Private Percy Hulme (West Street):

> 'I am writing as the bearer of very bad news for I am sorry to say that your son Percy was severely wounded last Saturday in action, … I am glad to say that up to the present as far as I can gather there is no fear of fatal results … . We were standing together when a shell burst close to us and I was rendered unconscious … . As far as I can ascertain your son was buried by sandbags … he was severely injured suffering from a wound in his abdomen and severely crushed … I can assure you I feel his loss greatly.'

That letter was received on the 9 October. Three days later they got another letter to say that Percy had died.

As the year drew to a conclusion, the war had affected others in the town in a different way. Charles Vickers, tailors of 15 & 17 High Street, Crewe's oldest established business (excepting the LNWR), whose roots went back to 1843, ceased to trade in November owing to a greatly reduced turnover. Only a decade previously the son of the founder had expanded the business by commencing a ladies' department that, according to *Eardley's Crewe Almanack*, was 'rapidly growing after a most successful season'. In December, Ward Brothers, another of the town's long established enterprises, went into voluntary liquidation, partially through the military commandeering their horses in August 1914.

Despite sixteen months of war, much of Crewe's communal life, though severely curtailed, continued to operate. Church services were held in the thirty-four churches and chapels that catered for the religious needs of the people by means of Sunday services and weeknight activities. Sixteen different Friendly Societies were functioning, some having a number of Lodges (Odd Fellows had twenty) attracting mainly male clientele. Drinking hours had been reduced by government regulations, yet over seventy pubs were still serving, with women often being the licensees, in cases where their husbands had responded to the call to the colours. Billiards, football, golf, cricket and bowls were just five sports that were regularly played. Pat Collin's fun-fair appeared, as usual, on the waste ground in Flag Lane in the spring of 1915.

Hundreds of people visited a garden in Mablins Lane to see the yucca plant, which supposedly bloomed once every century. For the privilege of viewing, a total of nearly £8 was collected by the householder for war charities. Donkinson's Oak was burned down, leaving Crewe with a name on a Crosville bus timetable but no visible remains of the tree. A measles' epidemic further blemished the closing weeks of the year, causing fifteen deaths in December, which included three children in one family. The parents of those three children, in Alfred Street, would feel the loss as keenly as if they had been killed in action.

Chapter Three

1916 Fighting for British Freedom

'What [Tommy] goes through here is for the sake of those he left behind, for the sake of British freedom and honour. Therefore he does it all with a good and willing heart.' Letter home from Jack Williamson (Cheshire Regiment) *Crewe Chronicle*, 11 March 1916

AT THE BEGINNING of the New Year 1916, it was reported that a Crewe nurse had been mentioned in one of Sir John French's dispatches. This must have been sometime in 1915, as French was recalled in December of that year to be replaced as Commander in Chief by Sir Douglas Haig. The nurse in question, who had joined the Territorial Nursing Service in 1912, was Sister E. Dodd, the daughter of Henry Dodd, a plumber of West Street. She had been in France since September 1914, where her bravery and heroism had been noted when she refused to leave her patients despite an imminent attack by the Germans.

The holiday season, such as it was in this second Christmas of the war, was exceptionally quiet in the town, according to contemporary comments. The Ram's Head, in Mill Street, could not have been quieter, for the landlady had surrendered the license,

German soldiers waiting for a troop train to transport them to somewhere in France in July 1916.

as her husband was a prisoner of war. A few weeks later the premises were sold for £160. Inclement weather added to the gloom for most families, who mainly spent their Christmas at home, as there were very few organized functions or parties. One soldier, stationed in France, remarked that his festive season was spent in the trenches, where he sent Fritz a few 'iron rations' for his Christmas dinner, which he hoped were enjoyed. No football now in No Man's Land or carol singing to mark a temporary truce.

A paragraph in the *Chronicle* early in 1916 notes an incident that, according to Richard Holmes in his *Acts of War*, was not uncommon. Two Crewe men, Privates T.H. Palin and W.J. Elson, were buried side by side by their comrades in the Cheshire Regiment, where they still lie as neighbours in Rifle House Cemetery, Belgium, in graves iv G13 and 14. It would seem that the close comradeship of war exercised fraternal care even when life was over. No such courtesies could be offered to Private W. Needham (Derby Street), who was killed by a shell burst a few days later and has no known grave.

It was soon discovered that the Derby scheme, introduced in 1915, had left 651,000 single men unattested out of 3.4 million nationally. Apparently the rural and semi-rural areas had not responded well. The originator of the scheme commented:

'The sense of unfairness thus created and the inequality of treatment of farmers has been most detrimental in these areas. The farmer ... is not a starred man but there are numerous cases of his sons and labourers being starred as cowmen and horsemen though in many instances it is known that they are not really so.'

If a man was starred it reduced his chances of being called to serve in the forces. About five hundred applications were received by the Crewe Tribunal for star status, only 10 per cent of which were accepted. When one considers the number of Crewe men that had volunteered, this rural reluctance was ammunition for those who wanted compulsory conscription. It was the apparent unfairness that motivated those who urged compulsion, rather than the need for more soldiers.

Supporters of compulsory conscription got their wish when, in January 1916, the Military Service Act was passed, with exemptions for those who could present cogent reasons why they could not serve. The very thought of compulsion was anathema to some, as was witnessed by the meeting in the Co-operative Hall, in Cooperative Street, called by the local branch of the National Union of Railwaymen. Amidst much shouting and uproar the speakers, Mr A. Bellamy, President of the NUR and an MP named Wardle, did their best to make themselves heard, though all to no avail. The reporter's comment was, 'and so closed one of the most disorderly meetings in Crewe for several years.' This is not to suggest that the town was equally divided in its opinion, as a careful reading of the local papers would confirm that the prevailing wish was for conscription.

Immediately the Military Service Act became operational, there was a flood of applications from men seeking exemption. Crewe Town Council was charged with the responsibility of creating a tribunal to decide cases, which they carried out by the simple expedient of changing the name of the existing Derby Scheme tribunal. Consequently, the fate of the appellants was decided by a body of politically motivated old men. Organized Labour immediately protested that the panel had no representation from the working class, a complaint that was rectified by the nomination of John Herring and

George Wilkinson, both supporters of the young Labour Party. The main objections to military service were that a business would suffer or that religious principles would be offended. The former was accepted far more often by tribunals than the latter, where men were asked '... if they saw their mother being killed would they help her.' Two brothers, who were members of the local Christadelphian Church, were taken off by the military after refusing service in the Red Cross.

An editorial in the *Chronicle* again complained that the tribunal for the rural area of south Cheshire was favouring farm workers to the extent of twenty-two exemptions out of twenty-four applications. This editorial went on to say that, 'Nantwich rural tribunal has acquired an ill-fame by exercising an extremely generous view when considering the needs of agriculture against the needs of the army.' Some of the reasons offered by Crewe men for exemption were 'a van-man on wholesale work', or 'responsibility for eighty-six horses' and, perhaps the most trivial, 'a bill-poster'.

Young men not in uniform often suffered the taunts and jibes of those who had volunteered. The local papers printed not a few letters from serving Crewe men criticizing the number of civilians available for military service, especially if there had been industrial action for higher pay. This attitude was particularly cruel when the object of ridicule wanted to be in uniform. Even as early as March 1915, a special badge was struck for LNWR workers, in reserved occupations, to prevent insults being levied against them by the young ladies of the town. In the spring of 1916, a local man, Albert E. Brookes, of the Cheshire Regiment, who had been repatriated after suffering severe injuries at Mons, committed suicide after being ridiculed for cowardice and not doing his duty. As mention was made in Parliament about this incident, it could have been a factor in the approval of a badge by the King and Army Council bearing the legend, 'For King and Empire Services Rendered' to be worn by soldiers wounded on active service.

Despite regulations being in place locally, indicating how to act to enemy aircraft flying over, nothing was done on the night of 31 January 1916, when a Zeppelin airship

The front cover of *Zeppeline über England*, a sardonic volume published in Germany in 1916 lauding the achievements of the Zeppelin. Aerial bombardment of towns and cities was a new departure in war, which became all too common in succeeding wars.

passed above Crewe. This was an actual incident, not a rumour, which, as we have seen, caused Winifred Heap to hide under the stairs in Heathfield Avenue. Another of Crewe's authors, Harry Hoff (pen-name William Cooper), described the incident in his memoirs *From Early Life*:

> 'The subject of this recollection is a Zeppelin. I remember being got up from sleep, taken down to the front door, and told to look up at the sky …. . I can see the arch of a starless black sky from beyond the roof of the house across the road to immediately overhead; and I can actually hear a throbbing sound in the sky …. . Yet I simply cannot see the thing itself! Next day we heard where the bombs had been dropped: [at] Madeley, ten or fifteen miles away.'

At the Council meeting following this, there was an enquiry as to why there had been no warning, with the Deputy Mayor J.H. Kettell, suggesting that somebody had been negligent. A warning system had been devised that included sounding the LNWR Works buzzer, along with the electrical engineer cutting the power to the town's lamps. As none of this happened, Councillor J. Madeley complained that workmen were prevented from obtaining a glass of beer when they came off work at 6.00 am, yet nobody could warn the town when enemy aircraft were overhead.

The fact that men could not get a drink at 6.00 am was the result of a massive reduction in licensing hours, ordered by the government under the Defence of the Realm Act (DORA). Such a move had been suggested locally in September 1914 by the

This picture, from *Zeppeline über England*, has the caption 'Der Zeppelinunterricht in einer Londoner schule' which freely translated is 'The Zeppelin lessons in a London school'.

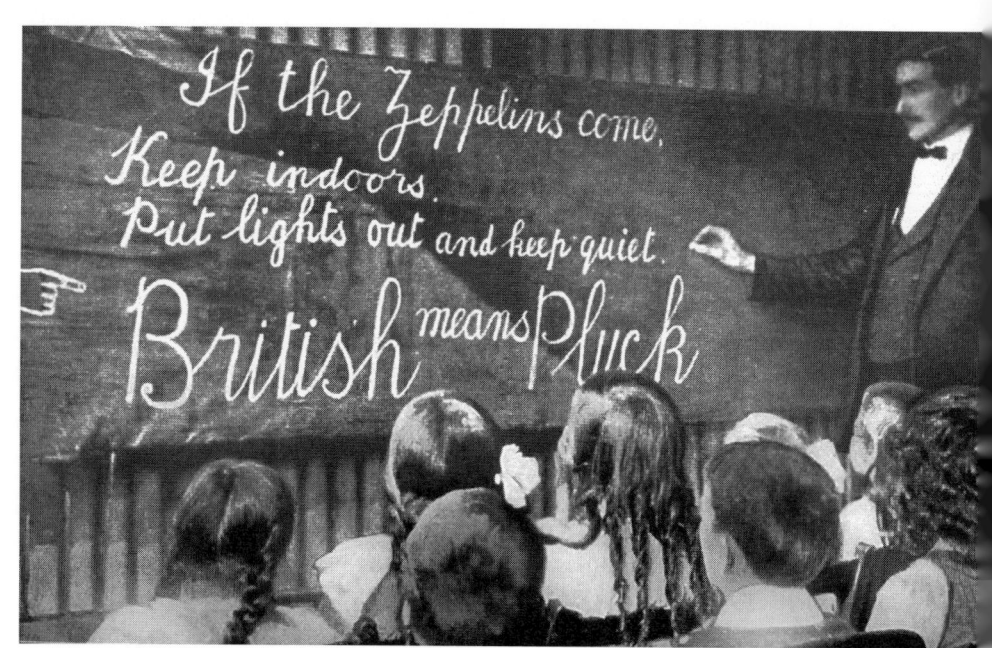

licensing committee, only to be rejected by the Council. Eighteen months into the war, pubs opened at 12 noon for two and a half hours. In the evening they closed at 9.30 pm, after only three hours of drinking time. Another element of these regulations was the prohibition of treating or buying drinks for men in uniform. The managers of the Brunswick and the Royal Hotel were just two of those prosecuted and fined, for allowing such practices. This curtailment of the consumption of alcohol resulted in a decline in convictions for drunkenness from seventy-three in 1914 to fifty-two the following year, a fall of 28 per cent.

Cigarettes were eagerly received by the troops, as many letters indicate. John Hough, of Lockett Street, a private in the King's Shropshire Light Infantry, wrote to thank the Dale Fund for a gift of 1000 cigarettes received early in 1916. Many miles further away, in the Middle East, Captain E.G. Hodgkison of the 7th Cheshires, gratefully acknowledged the safe receipt of two half hundred weight cases containing tobacco and cigarettes. Thirty-three prisoners of war from Crewe were not forgotten, for they received a thousand cigarettes and pounds of pipe tobacco. Private James Ganner (Grosvenor Street), a grateful recipient of some of this largess, sent a note expressing his gratitude.

Meanwhile, trench warfare continued to take its toll during the early months of 1916, despite the absence of set battles. Amongst the men of Crewe lost in this way, was Private William G Needham of the King's Shropshire Light Infantry, killed by a shell near Ypres on the 11 February. Aged 28, he had been in France for only four months, though he had enlisted in May 1915. Previously he had worked in the North Sheds. Eighteen-year-old Private Reginald Lightfoot (Brooklyn Street) was shot by a sniper while serving with the 19th Royal Fusiliers (2nd Public Schools). He was employed in the Town Council's electrical department. If he had lived a few weeks longer he could well have been commissioned, for his battalion was transferred to GHQ late in February, before being broken up. Such are the fortunes of war.

Second Lieutenant Harold Mansfield (1st Cheshire Regiment) was hit by a sniper while observing German trench activity. One month later, on the 12 April, he died from his wounds, just three months after receiving his commission. Lance Sergeant George Parsons (Reid Street), machine gun section of the King's Shropshire Light Infantry, was killed by a shell when standing by the entrance to his dug-out. He was just 21, having joined up before finishing his apprenticeship as a fitter/turner. Another youth, who was even younger when he enlisted, being only 16, was Rifleman W. Tench (Lawton Street), killed on 28 April 1916.

Among the men in the Council's employ who volunteered early in 1915, was R.S. Lewis, of the Army Sanitary Corps. One year later, he wrote an informative letter to his old boss, William Urquhart, describing how he managed to provide baths for front line troops. Apparently he had constructed a number of wooden tubs within a crude shed, about twenty minutes' walk from the trenches. In his letter he made the claim that almost 300 men could bathe and change their clothes between 9.00 am and 5.00 pm. Owing to the terminal ill-health of Urquhart, Richard Lewis was released by the War Office, at the request of the Council, so that he could resume his job as Sanitary and Nuisance Inspector, at Crewe, in May 1916. This was despite claiming previously that 'he would

The Sailors' and Soldiers' Rest was situated on Nantwich Road about one hundred yards from the railway station. Any serviceman changing trains at Crewe could always find a bed or a hot meal at the Rest.
(Mary and Colin Maclean)

not be an able-bodied man of military age at home for anything.' For those interested in the history of Crewe, Urquhart was originally given the job of Sanitary Inspector when he was discharged from the Works during the Intimidation Affair in 1889.

One of the changes introduced during 1916 that is still with us is the day light saving measures of altering the clock twice a year. This action, which was first introduced by the Germans, received the Royal Assent in May. A few months previous to this, the Council had introduced a government scheme for saving

A page from *Eardley's Magazine* showing the accounts of the Sailors' and Soldiers' Rest. Wilmot Eardley was a local printer with premises on Chester Bridge. He also published the Crewe Almanack between 1869 and 1917.

EARDLEY'S MAGAZINE

actual cost, and should a man whose only possession is an empty stomach tumble in, he is not turned away hungry. Many are also given monetary assistance.

FIRST HALF-YEARLY BALANCE SHEET
To Oct. 23rd, 1915.

Receipts	£	s.	d.
By Subscriptions	235	11	1½
,, Sale of Food and Tobacco	448	19	3½
,, Sale of old material, &c.	2	8	8
,, Bank Interest	0	5	0
Balance	£687	4	1

Expenditure	£	s.	d.
To Bread	37	18	0
,, Groceries	74	5	3
,, Ham	86	1	2
,, Meat Pies	42	9	0
,, Cakes	40	8	4
,, Fruit & Chocolate	20	7	6
,, Milk	10	7	8
,, Mineral Waters	20	10	0
,, Eggs	29	18	0
,, Tobacco & Matches	34	18	8
,, Laundry	2	5	7
,, Wages	51	8	8
,, National Health Insurance	0	6	3
,, Fire and Employers' Liability Insurances	3	2	11
,, Tobacco Licence	0	6	6
,, Furnishing	129	5	6
,, Maintenance of Building	12	19	8
,, Printing, Stationery, and Advertising	4	17	3
,, Postage and Receipt Stamps	0	10	5
,, Bank Commission and Cheque Books	1	8	0
,, Men in need	1	7	7
Balance	£605	1	11
	£82	2	2
Total	£687	4	1

This gives an idea of the counter trade and an indirect of the utility of the establishm

The Rest has now become an stitution, permanent so long as war lasts, and built upon a basi benevolent spirit which will be normal times are once again stored. It still appeals to the g erous consideration of the tow people, for if the Rest is to contin its sphere of usefulness, its financ soundness must be maintain The people should be encouraged give, by the commendable exam of the children, who have made a sold small articles to provide ciga ettes, and flowers, and by the spi of helpfulness shown by the Bo Scouts, who do duty night aft night at the Rest. The promote have reason to be grateful to t Railway Company, who have helpe in many ways, and supplied gratu tously the gas for heating an cooking and electricity for lighting The happy countenances of thos who gather round the tables mus be sufficient compensation for thos who have given or worked for th good of the Rest, and we can bes describe the homely atmosphere o the surroundings in the words o Cowper:—

Let the curtains fall, wheel the sofa round,
And while the bubbling and loud-hissing urn
Throws up a steaming column, and the cups
That cheer but not inebriate wait on each,
So let us welcome peaceful evening in.

power, along with its effect as an air raid precaution, by switching off all street lamps early in the evening. Obviously, as this left the streets in darkness, many accidents ensued, including a councillor who received a black eye by walking into a lamp-post. As the regulations also compelled tradesmen and residents to subdue the lights in their shops or houses, further trouble broke out. Alderman Kettell refused to suppress the intensity of his internal lights, or to cover his windows with blinds. He claimed the lighting law was a farce and if he had his way the whole of Crewe would keep its lights on. Along with eight other shopkeepers he was fined twenty shillings plus costs.

Not all of the men in uniform were heroes, as is proved by the number of cases where men did not return to their units after being on leave. In April 1916, Private J.G. Reeves (South Street) and Private James Rogerson (Peter Street) were sent back to their regiments under escort, after being arrested in the same week while hiding in Crewe. When Private J. Kinnick of Gresty Terrace was traced and arrested for being absent without leave, the policeman who tracked him was awarded a ten shillings bonus. Arthur Evans (not of Crewe) absent from 2/2nd Lovat Scouts, stole £6-0-0 from the reception desk at the Sailors' and Soldiers' Rest, on Nantwich Road, in November 1915. Unfortunately for him, the sharp eyed receptionist recognized him when he visited again in May 1916, and called the police. The first case of enforced enlistment under the Military Service Act occurred in April, when Joseph Walters of Sheppard Street was charged with being an absentee. His appeal had been turned down, yet after Lieutenant Lindsay Jones, of the recruiting office, graciously granted him more time, he still refused to serve. He was fined £2-0-0 before being handed over to the Military Police.

At the end of May, the greatest sea battle of the war took place in the North Sea, the Battle of Jutland. In total two hundred and fifty ships were drawn up in the only full scale clash of sea armour in the four years of hostilities. Words will not be used to describe the long and complex manoeuvres, under the direction of Admiral Jellicoe and Vice Admiral David Beatty, other than to say that the British fleet lost fourteen ships and the Germans eleven. Both sides claimed a victory, though a better judgment would be a draw and a British strategic victory as the German High Seas fleet never put out to sea again. Amongst the men drowned and the ships that sank, were Samuel Moorhouse (Nile Street), HMS *Indefatigable*, William Walker (Exchange Street), Frederick Cooke (Cotterill Street) and Arthur Bradley (Moss Square), aged 21, all on HMS *Defence*. A fellow sailor (not a Crewe man) on HMS *Defence* was Cecil Abercrombie, an international rugby player and county cricketer. On HMS *Durham* was the 17-year-old Bernard Grimshaw Ineson, a boy telegraphist, whose death added more sorrow to his

After an apprenticeship as a carpenter, Singleton Charnock eventually served on the *Queen Mary*, which was sunk at the Battle of Jutland. He was one of over 1200 sailors from that ship that lost their lives.

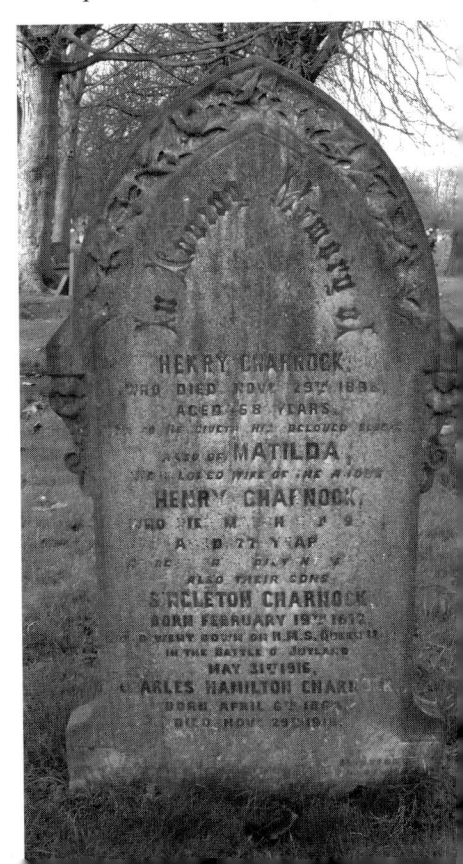

mother Gertrude, a widow of Ruskin Road. These are just five of the nine or so Crewe men who went to a North Sea grave at the Battle of Jutland.

Six days into June, the nation was shaken with the news that HMS *Hampshire*, fresh from the Battle of Jutland, had struck a mine off the Orkney Islands, with Lord Kitchener, the Secretary of State for War on board. Very few were saved when the *Hampshire* sank about fifteen minutes after being holed; Kitchener was not among them, meaning that the man who had motivated so many to enlist in the heady summer days of 1914 would not witness his volunteer army being severely damaged at the Battle of the Somme. Two of the Artificer Engineers on the *Hampshire* were Crewe men, Matthew Hobson of Richard Moon Street and Cuthbert Fincken. Both of these men were lost, as was Sir H.F. Donaldson, an ex-pupil of Frances Webb at Crewe.

Social life in the town continued, especially for those who were not mourning the death of a son or husband. In June, the controversial film *The Birth of a Nation* was shown to full houses at the Theatre, every afternoon and evening for a week. The advert for this covered virtually the whole of the front page of the *Crewe Chronicle*. In the weeks after Easter, the Irish Rebellion was reported at length, including a letter from the Crewe Irish League deploring the action in Dublin. Perhaps a more representative view of the serving Irishman was recorded in the visitor's book of the Crewe Sailors' and Soldiers' Rest in 1919.

'We are not all Sinn Feiners so think of the Irish lads that fought and fell in this great war for freedom for small nations. So think on if Ireland gets her freedom we (the Irish) are the first boys in the field to fight in the next great war.'

The remarks were penned by Paddys Dillon and O'Brien.

A scandal that was discussed around the home fires in the spring of 1916 was the libel case, brought by the Vicar of Christ Church, the Reverand Walter Bidlake, against a Mrs Emma Fulham, who he charged with publishing a defamatory libel by writing over one hundred letters saying that he was her husband by 'covenant of God'. He was awarded £88-0-0 damages when he won the case, while she was detained at His Majesty's pleasure.

A farewell celebration was arranged in the Mechanics' Institution for W.W.H. Warneford, the Works manager, on his transfer to Earlestown. According to contemporary reports, over four thousand people subscribed towards his leaving presents. Warneford's son Walter was an officer on board Airship NS 11 when it was lost in 1919. His more famous relative,

The programme for a concert marking the transfer of W.W.H. Warneford from Crewe to Earlestown in 1916. His son Walter was killed over the Norfolk coast in 1919 when piloting airship NS11. Four years earlier, in June 1915, Reginald Warneford (cousin to Walter) won the VC for 'downing' a Zeppelin.

George William Sparrow (Oakley Street) is standing first from the left in this group of teachers at Adelaide Street School in 1914. Later he became a member of RE Special Brigade, which was responsible for the British Army's chemical war effort. He was killed in action near Ypres on 30 June 1916.

Reginald, won the VC in aerial combat with a Zeppelin, before he was killed in June 1915.

After twenty-three months of hostilities, such locations as Mons, the Marne, the Aisne, La Bassée, Messines, Ypres, Loos, Gallipoli, Palestine and Salonika had lodged in the national psyche. In July 1916, there was fought a battle that was to provide a name which remains forever an English epithet for a military disaster. Known colloquially, to the soldiers who participated in it, as the 'big push', it was planned as a joint operation between the French and the British. Owing to the German attack upon Verdun, in February, Sir Douglas Haig, now Commander in Chief of the BEF, was responsible for supplying the lion's share of fighting men, which he accomplished by providing eleven divisions in Rawlinson's Fourth Army, aided by two with Allenby's Third Army. Added to these were six divisions of French troops.

On 1 July, at 7.30 am thousands of young men of Kitchener's Army and the Territorials, who had volunteered many months before, climbed from their front line to walk slowly across No Man's Land, to occupy trenches that had ostensibly been cleared of the enemy by a massive artillery barrage. Unfortunately, along the majority of the attack zone of roughly 18 miles, the German defences had not been wiped out and the attackers were met by a stream of bullets and artillery shells. As is well known, 1 July 1916, was the black day of the British Army, with almost sixty thousand casualties. This was the first day of the Somme.

On Monday 3 July, the *Times* used such sub-headings as: 'Forward in the West', 'Start of a Great Attack', 'Day Goes Well' to describe the first day's fighting. Within the report it was said that the British had broken through on a front of 7 miles to a depth of 1000 yards, over running the German trenches. In addition, the villages of Mametz, Montauban and Fricourt were occupied by soldiers of General Rawlinson's Fourth Army. The *Crewe Chronicle* and the *Crewe Guardian* sounded the same optimistic note, as they, like the *Times*, could only use the official war office communiqué. What none of the reports mentioned, partly because the army itself did not know until 4 or 5 July, was the fifty eight thousand casualties suffered that first day, around one third of them dead. Amongst these were three Crewe men: Private A. Cartwright (Evans Street) of the Cheshires, Private Joseph H. Yardley (Chesterfield Street), 2nd Battalion Manchester Regiment; and Private T.C. Evans (Brown Street), of the King's Liverpool Regiment. By the end of July, around another three dozen soldiers from Crewe had been added to the list of the fallen.

To give an account of all of those from the town who fell that month would take up more space than is available, so the following are but examples of those brave men who had marched off to war 'as if it were a game' to quote Sir Ian Hamilton's words. Amongst the many wounded on the first day of the campaign was Lance Corporal H. Holloway (Alton Street), Queen Victoria's Rifles. This battalion was part of the 56th (London) Division which, along with the 46th (North Midland) Division was responsible for a diversionary attack upon Gommercourt at the northern flank of the fighting. During that first day the 56th Division suffered the price of 4,314 casualties, one of whom was the lance corporal from Crewe who had previously been wounded at Hill 60 in Belgium in 1915.

Walter Broughton (Martin Street), a private in the South Lancs, who enlisted in August 1914 from the LNWR copper-shop, was killed in action six days after the start of the battle. He had written in October 1915 that he hoped to '… come out of this lot triumphantly with a medal on my chest.' Sadly, it was not to be. Private Alec Harrison (Glover Street), of the Cheshires, was last seen digging near some unexploded shells on 5 September, near to High Wood. His death, which was confirmed in July 1917, meant that Crewe Co-operative Society lost another employee. Private Charles Nield, aged 25, of the Royal Engineers, was wounded then shipped back to the UK, where he died in a military hospital. His funeral was held in Coppenhall Church, though, unlike the Villiers Russell twins, few councillors were present. A soldier's death was common place in 1916.

1 July was just the beginning of a campaign that continued until the middle of November, meaning that many more men were killed. Twenty-one days into the operation on the Somme optimistic notes were still being sounded, as can be read in a *Crewe Guardian* leader:

'Nearly three weeks have passed since the opening of the great offensive movement of the Allies on the Western Front. During this time substantial progress has been made … the tide appears to have turned in favour of the Allies into whose grasp the offensive has surely passed.'

The following week, a comment was added that emphasized that all was going well with the offensive battle so brilliantly opened on the first day of the month.

Many words have been devoted to the fighting on the Somme because it is popularly seen as the archetypal battle of the Great War. Altogether approximately 18 per cent of all the Great War names recorded on the war memorial on Municipal Square, were killed in the bitter fighting on the Somme. Perhaps a few more names from the war memorials erected around Crewe, will help to reinforce this point.

Second Lieutenant G.F. Woodhouse of the South Lancs was killed in action on 10 July. At six feet three inches, yet only 19, he had spent his childhood on the Corporation Farm, leaving Manchester University to enlist. The previous day, another commissioned officer, George Cumming, also aged 19, the son of a Crewe retail chemist, was numbered with the dead on the Somme. Five weeks later, Private Frank Dean (formerly a mechanic at Cooke's Nantwich Road Garage), was buried in Blighty Valley Cemetery after only six weeks at the Front. Ernest Riley, of Chesterfield Street, who had already received notice of the death of a son (Edward) killed in action in November 1914, now learned that another son, Arthur, of the Royal Welsh Fusiliers had died, on 15 of July, attacking Bazentin, near Delville Wood. Attached to the same battalion, and fighting in the same attack, was the war poet Robert Graves, friend of Siegfried 'Mad Jack' Sassoon, also of the RWF and engaged in the same struggle. Private Thomas Clayton, of the 1/10th King's Liverpool who had enlisted at Crewe in December 1915, was killed near to Guillemont on the 13 August, four days after his Medical Officer Captain Noel Chavasse won his first VC for carrying in the wounded of Clayton's battalion.

Another Somme victim was a former employee of Crewe Co-operative Society, Private W.L. Cheshire (King's Liverpool Regiment), who died of wounds in an English hospital. Consequently, after a service at the Edleston Road United Methodist Church, he was buried in Crewe Cemetery. Guardsman Thomas Dutton was fighting with the Grenadiers in September when he was killed, the day before one of his officers, Raymond Asquith died, after being shot in the chest. Many visitors to the battlefields stop to gaze at the grave of Asquith, as he was the son of the Prime Minister. Guardsman Dutton was an unknown, from Crewe, so sadly does not warrant the same attention, especially as he has no known grave,

Grave of Private William Cheshire of the King's Liverpool Regiment, who died of wounds received at the Battle of the Somme in July 1916. Previous to enlisting, he worked for Crewe Co-operative Society as a counter assistant.

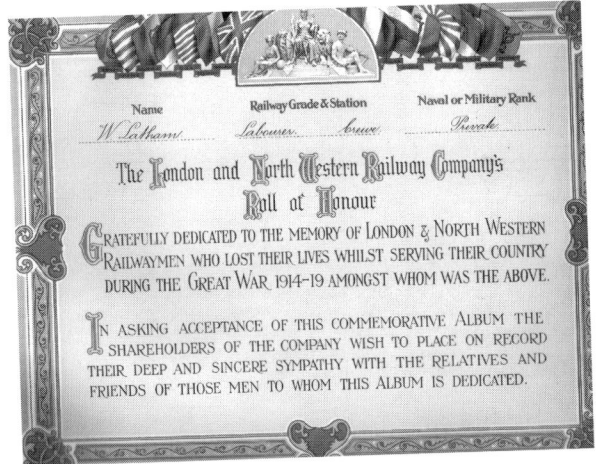

though his name is recorded on the Thiepval Memorial.

In July, while Crewe men were fighting on the Somme, the arch-recruiter and editor of *John Bull* (a weekly magazine), Horatio Bottomley visited Crewe as the main attraction at a rally in the Town Hall. Alderman J.H. Kettell, who presided at the crowded meeting, described him as 'one of England's greatest orators'. Others, less enamoured, called him a demagogue. George Howes, night manager at the Crewe Arms Hotel during this period, describes (in his unpublished memoirs) an encounter with Bottomley:

'I remember on one occasion the notorious Horatio Bottomley staying in the Hotel along with his secretary. He had been addressing a meeting locally. I had occasion to go into his room and they had a pile of money on the table which they were counting, the proceeds of his lecture I suppose.'

LNWR Roll of Honour, which contains the name of every employee who fell in battle. This volume was dedicated to Private W. Latham, killed fighting in Delville Wood with the King's Shropshire Light Infantry (KSLI) during the Battle of the Somme in August 1916.

Bottomley, who often charged a large fee for his platform appearances, was imprisoned in 1922 for fraud. As a corollary to this, F.B. Meyer, an internationally recognized Christian preacher, addressed a meeting in the Town Hall, which was claimed to be the first time that Anglicans and nonconformists had officially met together in Crewe. The war was breaking down barriers.

A local man, whose expressed opinions were opposed to those of the aforementioned demagogue, was Edwin Yates, of Ernest Street, and a Labour Councillor, elected in 1911. Sometime in the summer of 1916, he contradicted a letter, from the Women's Imperial Defence Council, stating that '… we cannot do without Germany.' Instantly he was ridiculed by Alderman Kettell, who claimed it rankled his mind for any man to speak of showing brotherly kindness to Germany. John Williams, a fellow Labour councillor, added his voice to the outcry against Yates. In reply Yates wrote:

'The preaching of hatred and revenge is so dangerous and a settlement dictated by vindictiveness is so fraught with terrible consequences to the future of the world that to appeal to something higher and nobler is surely not pro-German.'

Yates was ploughing a lone furrow, for it was impossible for him to find much support locally for his views, however politically sensible they were in the long run. Much of the peace settlement of 1919, engineered in a spirit of spite and vengeance, was partially responsible for the rise of Hitlerism and the resumption of the conflict in 1939.

The mid-summer of 1916 also witnessed a letter from Whitehall criticizing the level of juvenile crime in the town. Along with Birkenhead, Crewe had the highest level of offending by children in Cheshire. Actually this was nothing new, as the same two towns had been singled out in 1876 as '… the two great seats of juvenile crime in the county.' School attendance was also poor, which must have been a factor in the crime figures. Some commentators placed the responsibility upon the mothers neglecting the family while the husband was in the forces. Whatever the cause, there are many cases that illustrate the criticism, such as two brothers aged 10 and 12, of Bulkeley Street, who stole a lady's cycle, for which they each received several strokes of the birch rod. Two other boys received similar punishment the same month, for stealing toffee from a stall in the market.

The second anniversary of the war called forth a massive crowd on the Market Square to witness the mayor and corporation filling a makeshift platform as the volunteers and boy scouts followed the Crewe Works Band on to the Square. Also present was Bowen Cooke, the LNWR's Chief Mechanical Engineer, and Ernest Craig, MP. Patiently, the crowd listened to the speeches, especially the resolution that was approved by acclamation. This promised that 'On this second anniversary of a righteous war… Crewe records an inflexible determination to continue to victorious end the struggle to maintain ideas of liberty and justice …'. Less than two weeks after this resolution was passed, Private Charles Stelfox, of Underwood Lane, was the next Crewe man to be killed playing his part in that struggle for liberty.

Back in Cheshire, some of the workers were using their liberty to try to extract cost of living advances from their employers. In October, a group of men, working on a new sewage system, went on strike when the council refused to advance their wages from

LNWR fitting shop in the Old Works, where Alfred Cartwright (Brown Street) was working before he joined the KSLI. He was killed in action on 3 April 1916.

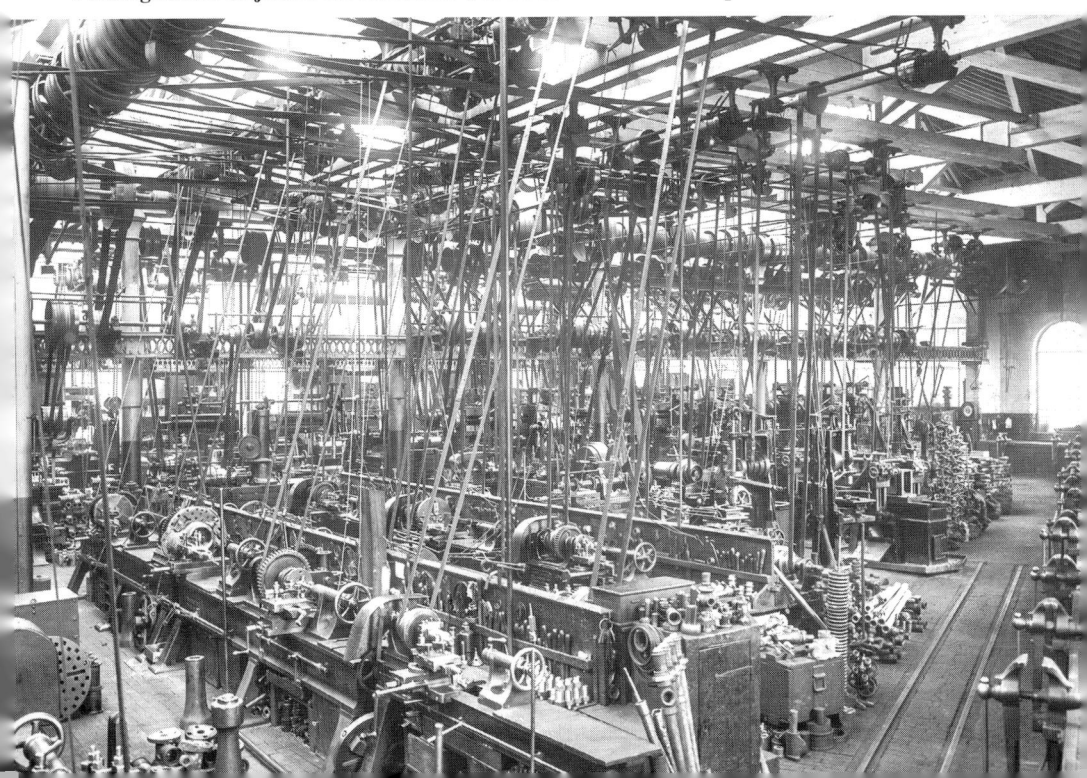

twenty shillings a week to twenty-three shillings. Before negotiations began, the council committee responsible had a long discussion about whether to recognize the men's union. The *Chronicle*'s attitude to this militancy was: '… an ideal shop assistant is the man who uncomplainingly works from 8.30 in the morning to 7.30 in the evening, who does not belong to a mischief making union and who is willing to surrender a day's holiday in war time.' Despite this diatribe, the proprietors of the *Chronicle* raised the price of their newspaper by 50 per cent. That the cost of living had risen and was continuing to do so was incontrovertible. A letter in the local press complained that even the barber had increased the price of haircuts from two pennies to four, and a penny shave now cost twice as much.

To cope with the increasing need for charitable giving, there was a flag day every week in the town, besides special efforts and continuing collections. One of the more unusual, though typically English, was the flag-day in October for 'Sick and Wounded Horses' that raised £127, a not inconsiderable amount until compared with the £140 raised in the much smaller town of Whitchurch for the same cause. About a fortnight later, Lord Roberts' Fund for Disabled Soldiers and Sailors was the cause of the week, and £240 worth of flags were purchased by the good people of Crewe. Also arranged in October, was the Red Cross Money Raising Day, when all the great and the good made an appearance at the events and stalls in the Town Hall. Such activities as a whist drive or a promenade concert were organized, with Crewe Works Military Band providing the music. A local auctioneer, E.H. Manley, conducted an auction sale of donated items, as varied as a chip-pan, bottles of whisky, a case of butterflies, four aspidistra plants, a live cockerel and pullet, two large pork pies and an Indian parrot in a cage. Altogether, £561 was accumulated for the Red Cross's war work.

Nationally, the major event at the close of the year was the replacement of Asquith as Prime Minister by David Lloyd George, while locally the Town Council was bringing all available land under cultivation for growing food, which was becoming scarce and expensive. Shortages of commodities were so intense that people were convicted for stealing a few potatoes.

As Christmas approached, George Eaton-Shore, the Borough Surveyor, died in his bed at his residence in Hungerford Road at the age of 60, the same week as his son John, aged 36, of the Royal Marines, was buried near to Varennes, killed in action. On Christmas Day, Josephine Brown, a widow of Market Terrace, received the dreaded telegram announcing that her son, Private Thomas Brown of the Cheshires, had been killed a few days previously. He was 19. Death, and news of death, was no respecter of holidays.

A Christmas card sent by St John's Anglican Church, Stalbridge Road, Crewe. This church, which was opened in 1892, was built mainly at LNWR expense, as were all of the Crewe Anglican churches of the Victorian era.
(Mary and Colin Maclean)

Chapter Four

1917 Another Year of Sacrifice

'What moral and scientific wealth has been mown down in this pitiless war. But our sacrifice has not been in vain.' Sapper G.H. Broadhurst of Crewe. *Crewe Chroncile,* 28 April 1917

AS BOTH FOOD and liquor were scarce, there was nothing to inculcate merry feelings, on New Year's Day in Crewe, neither was there much cause for celebration, as 1916 had ended with a sense of stalemate. Despite enormous casualties, the battle lines were little changed on the Western Front from those at the end of 1914. Many in the town must have wondered where victory was going to come from. There was even less reason for cheer in a home in Hungerford Road, when news came through a few days later that Rifleman J.B. Williams, of the 5th Battalion King's Liverpool Regiment, had been killed, along with four comrades, when a shell hit their dugout near Ypres on New Year's Day. Leaving a promising job as an engineer in the Permanent Way Department, in Gresty Road, Williams had enlisted in the rush to the colours in September 1914, when he was 24-years-old. The Vaughan family, of West Street, were mourning the death in Mesopotamia of Bombardier Walter Vaughan, who died on 15 December, 1916, from wounds in his head and back. He was buried in the Military Cemetery at Sinn Abtar. His father, a local preacher with the Primitive Methodists, and an ironmonger and builder, had been the town's mayor at the start of the war.

By January 1917 there were over sixty Crewe prisoners of war incarcerated in various camps in Germany. Some of them, such as Private Potts (New Street) and Private J. Hinde (Sefton Avenue), were moved to occupied Russia to work in the fields. We have seen in a previous chapter that a committee of LNWR employees took responsibility for sending food parcels to any of their enlisted fellow employees who had been captured by the enemy. It had been realised by government officials as early as 1915, that private enterprise distribution of victuals left some PoWs without any support. Consequently, a new system came into force when the Central Prisoners of War

Though published by the *Daily Telegraph*, this book was sold to raise funds for the French Red Cross. Edmund Dulac was a nationally recognized artist who illustrated books and even designed postage stamps and bank notes.

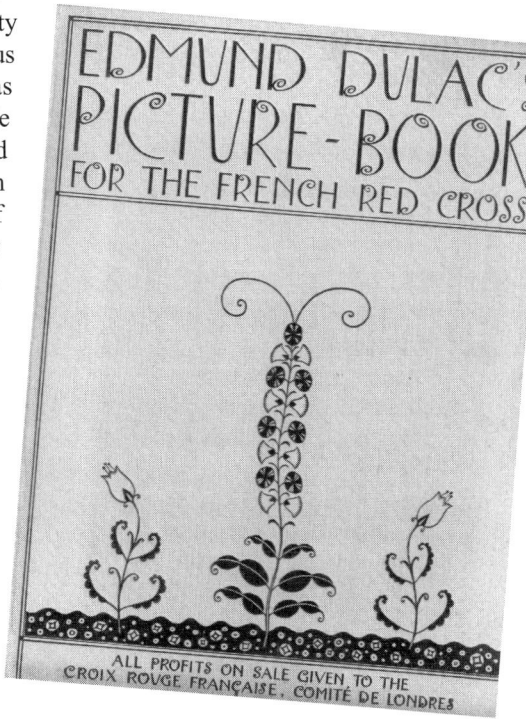

ROTE KREUZ-SAMMLUNG
1914
SAMMLUNG ZUGUNSTEN DER FREI-
WILLIGEN KRANKENPFLEGE IM KRIEGE

In a similar fashion to the UK and to France, the German Red Cross raised money for humanitarian purposes. This card was designed by Ludwig Hohlwein, a prolific German poster artist. (Fred Ikin)

Committee of the British Red Cross and Order of St John was established, with the sole power to authorize committees or associations to pack and dispatch parcels and to control such committees. Initially it was not popular, but gradually it was accepted when it was shown that some PoWs, without relatives or friends, received no parcels at all.

Crewe became affiliated as a packing centre for sixty-seven members of the Cheshire Regiment. The despatch rate was usually six parcels per man per month, each parcel costing six shillings, with thirteen pounds of bread baked in Copenhagen being allocated to each man. Joseph Davies (MP for Crewe from 1918) sponsored parcels for two Crewe PoWs. By December 1916, the employees committee had sent 1,000 food parcels and 120 clothes parcels. Over the next two years well over 5,000 parcels were despatched from Crewe, at a cost of approximately £3,000.

Some prisoners returned to the town before the end of hostilities, owing to a repatriation scheme for severely injured PoWs. Two (Privates Farrell and Moss) returned to their homes in Crewe, in July 1915. At the end of 1916, Private James Heeson of Leighton Street came back minus his right arm. Formerly a barman in the Grand Junction Hotel, he enlisted in the Royal Welsh Fusiliers almost at the declaration of hostilities. His menu in the PoW camp was a piece of bread, with a little grease and marmalade for breakfast, dinner was potatoes and kidney bean soup, tea the same as breakfast, while supper at 6.00 pm was more poor quality soup. Without the parcels they would have starved. Interestingly, a parcel meant for Private Heeson was returned from Germany in good condition after he had been repatriated. One soldier, Private W. Cannon of Alexander Street, successfully escaped from a PoW camp in the autumn of 1915.

Along with the ever present worry of the death or disablement of a son or husband fighting in one of the areas of conflict, there was also the shortage of food and coal to contend with. The mayor in 1917, Alderman J.H. Kettell, in his New Year message to the town, said that the duty of all not in the fighting forces was to do everything they possibly could to increase the food supply. By this time the war had been raging for nearly thirty months, so that it was only to be expected that there would be shortages. Lack of any system of rationing exacerbated the situation, as the better-

Eat Less Bread
—◼—
Waste None

Food propaganda leaflet published in 1917 to encourage the people to eat less bread, as by this date food was becoming quite scarce. The cause of this was the unrestricted U boat campaign, responsible for sinking thousands of tons of merchant shipping.

off could stock up their larders, leaving the shop shelves empty. In March 1917, the women's section of the local trades' council passed a resolution condemning government apathy in the face of blatant profiteering.

To rectify this, a local food control committee was established, with R. Holdaway, the Market Inspector, appointed as Food Controller, holding powers granted by the Food Control Order No 1, 1917. This brought about prosecution of local traders, such as George Smith of Ridgway Street, fined £3 for selling potatoes for a farthing more than the set price. He also required customers to purchase carrots in addition to potatoes. At that time there was a tremendous shortage of potatoes in Crewe, so much so that over two thousand people were queuing for them in the Market Hall in May. As the wealthy could still over-stock their shelves, the food control orders only remedied the blight of profiteering. Addressing the shortage of food, caused mainly by the unrestricted German U boat campaign, had to await the introduction of a rationing scheme in 1918.

One of the immediate answers to some shortages was to grow your own, which happened through the urging of the mayor and the council's allotment garden programme. This was channelled through the land cultivation sub-committee formed at the end of 1916. Initially, all spare land in the council's possession, including the site of the future Ludford Street School and the playing field of the school in Ruskin Road, was ploughed and planted. By the end of January over three hundred separate plots, covering land in West Street, Queen Street, Ruskin Road, Gainsborough Road, Hungerford Road, Bedford Street and Somerville Street, had been leased to individuals at one shilling per rood. Before the end of May allotments had been established at another twenty-five locations in the town. This meant that the by the end of the war over 2,200 private allotments were being tended, compared with less than 200 in 1914. The Town Council also encouraged householders to keep poultry, rabbits and even pigs, where they had sufficient space. In addition, Groby Farm, Coppenhall, was deemed inefficient and so was taken into the possession of the War Agricultural Committee for food production.

Many weird and wonderful suggestions were made to increase the availability of food, not least being the many recipes supplied by amateur cooks. The *Chronicle* printed

UNITED METHODIST CHURCH, HIGHTOWN, CREWE.

FOR PURPOSES OF

WAR ECONOMY

THE

ANNUAL TEA

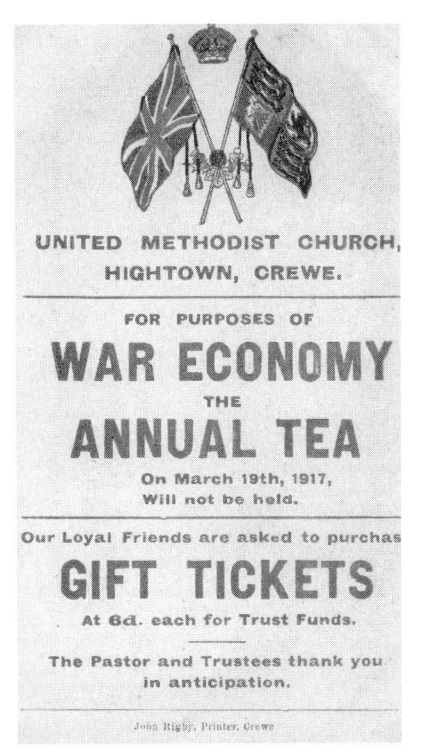

On March 19th, 1917, Will not be held.

Our Loyal Friends are asked to purchas

GIFT TICKETS

At 6d. each for Trust Funds.

The Pastor and Trustees thank you in anticipation.

John Rigby, Printer, Crewe

Acute shortage of food caused the cancellation of the annual tea at Hightown United Free Church. This building, known in later years as Heathfield, owing to its early association with Martin Heath, one of the town's fathers, has since been demolished.

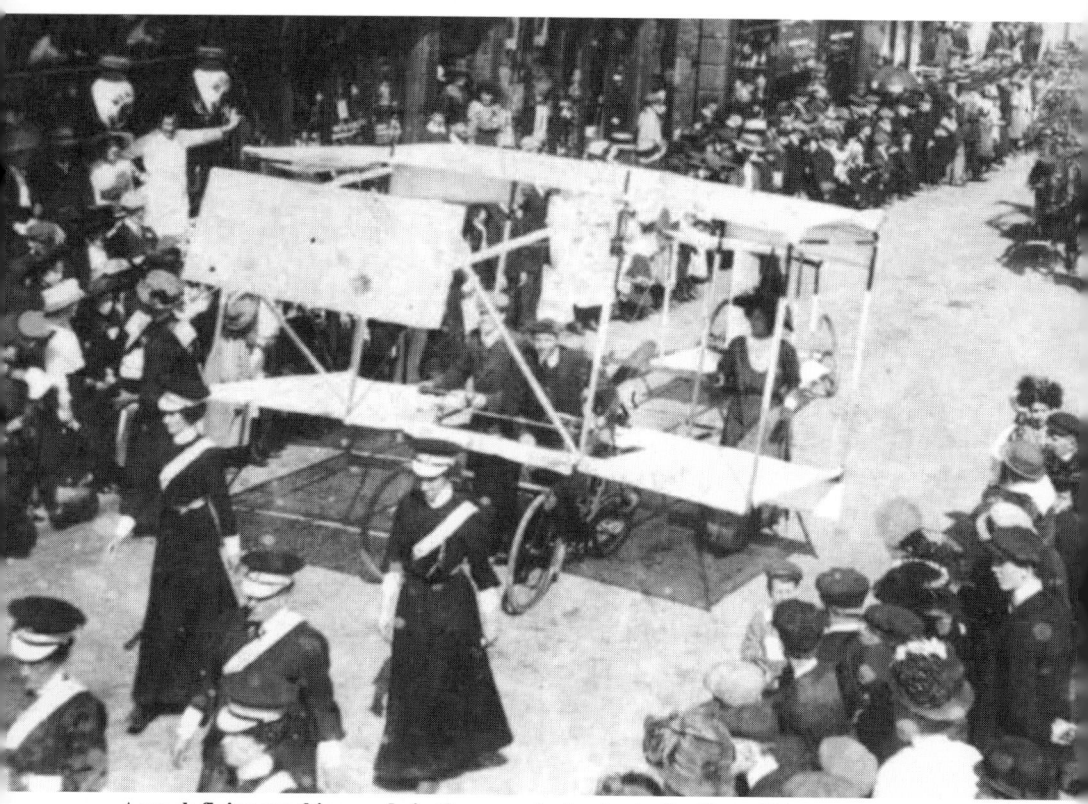

A mock flying machine made in the years just prior to the Great War as a feature in the annual fête to raise funds for the Cottage Hospital. Many of the men in this image would see service in the ranks when the war started. *(Mary and Colin Maclean)*

a formula for making a substitute for potatoes using cooked butter beans and rice, while an alternative for red meat could be produced by utilizing bacon and eggs, mixed with boiled and mashed beans. Because they were considered a pest that ate too much food, the council offered two shillings per hundred for dead sparrows or sparrow eggs. Perhaps the silliest advice was that given by Mrs Pender Reeves, National Director of Women's Services, who said that people should eat enough bread but not more than enough. As the problem was getting enough bread in the first place, her advice was plainly fatuous, as was her comment that it was disloyal to have indigestion. One would imagine that consumption of the proffered substitute food would cause acute indigestion.

Military operations on the Western Front in the first weeks of 1917 included localised fighting around the Ancre, a tributary of the Somme, in attempts to capture various German held trenches. Eleven days into 1917 Private John William Maddock, a Crewe man, who had been in the Manchester Regiment hardly six months, after leaving his job in the forge at Crewe Works, was shot by a sniper when carrying a message. On 11 February Private William Crabtree, serving with the Australian Infantry, died when he was shot in the chest. He emigrated to Australia from his home in Nantwich Road for a new life in agriculture, only to enlist when the call to the colours came when he was aged 17.

Deaths also occurred on other fronts, such as the shooting of 19-year-old Private Tom Dudley, of Cemetery Road (now Broad Street), when he attacked a Turkish trench along with others of his comrades in the Royal Welsh Fusiliers. Sergeant James Cartwright (Bright Street), who enlisted in the Loyal North Lancashire Regiment in August 1914 from the LNWR Signal Department, was killed in March 1917. Having no known grave he is but a name on a memorial panel in Basra. Gunner William Edge, who was also employed by the LNWR when he lived in Underwood Lane, died of wounds in a Glasgow Hospital, and was laid to rest in Coppenhall churchyard. For some it was only a matter of recovering from wounds or other disabilities. Second Lieutenant Charles Bullock, the son of Henry Bullock, one of the town's professional photographers, was sent home in February 1917 with shell shock. Sadly, on returning to his regiment he was killed in September 1918, in the advance that led to victory later that year. Private A. Nield (West Street), formerly a clerk in the General Offices of the LNWR, was in a Bradford hospital in January with frost-bite, a consequence of the bitter weather in France.

Heavy frosts were also the lot of people in Crewe in the first weeks of 1917, when the temperature dropped to 0 degrees F (-18° C), which froze the park lake, allowing skating for anyone inclined to pay the six pennies demanded by the council. All money raised was divided between the Red Cross Hospital at Webb's Orphanage and a Fund for Blind Soldiers and Sailors. The scarcity of coal to warm their homes must have been a factor in the rise of old people dying during this extremely cold snap. Early in March, after two nights of particularly severe frosts, the temperature rose, meaning the plumbers were busy repairing nearly a hundred burst water pipes. It must be remembered that most of the two dozen or so plumbers that advertised their services in pre-war days usually employed a man and a boy, a situation that had altered by 1917, when so many Crewe men were in the forces.

As a money raiser for the fifty bed Red Cross Auxiliary Hospital in the decade old, but under used, Webb's Orphanage, a War Relics exhibition was organized in February in the Mechanics' Institute. Amongst the exhibits were a piece of a Zeppelin, a wing off a German aeroplane, German machine guns captured at Courcelette during the Battle of the Somme, a trench mortar, field periscope, a German sniper's camouflage suit and various regimental badges. Fifteen hundred school children filed past, in addition to five

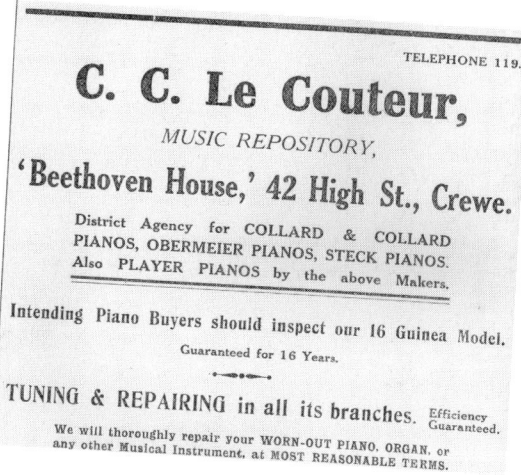

Gunner Jack Le Couteur of the Royal Garrison Artillery was killed in action, aged 20, in May 1917. Before enlisting he was training to be a draughtsman with the LNWR. The family business advertised regularly in Eardley's *Crewe Almanack*.

William Edge occupies one of the few Commonwealth War Graves in Coppenhall churchyard. He died of wounds in a Glasgow hospital and was buried here on what would have been his 30th birthday. His grave is about a quarter of a mile from his home in Underwood Lane.

thousand Crewe townspeople. Altogether the event raised just over £83.

In addition to the Red Cross Hospital, money had to be found for the Memorial Hospital in Victoria Avenue, and St John's Hospital in France that Crewe was supporting. In-patients at the Memorial Hospital totalled 638 in 1916, requiring some 6,658 visits by the town's doctors. Contributions from patients only amounted to £584, so much fund raising via the people of Crewe was necessary to fill the financial gap. Similarly, St John's Hospital in France, where Mary Warneford was a superintendent, needed supporting. Between May 1916 and June 1917 Doody's factory sent £60, Hammond & Co £28, a flag day in the town £253, the Cumberland Arms £19, Smethurst & Holden £15, various LNWR departments added another £17 which, along with small amounts from schools and another flag day, meant Crewe had subscribed well over £1200.

Awards for Crewe servicemen were proudly announced in the local papers whenever they occurred. Early in the New Year, Sergeant Herbert Farrington (Market Street) of the Cheshire Regiment was awarded a Military Medal for notable actions during the Battle of

Remains of two cups, dug up from a rubbish tip in Crewe, used in the Sailors' and Soldiers' Rest on Nantwich Road or by servicemen taking advantage of the mobile canteen as they passed through the station. The abbreviation CEMS stood for Church of England Men's Society. *(Mick Kelly)*

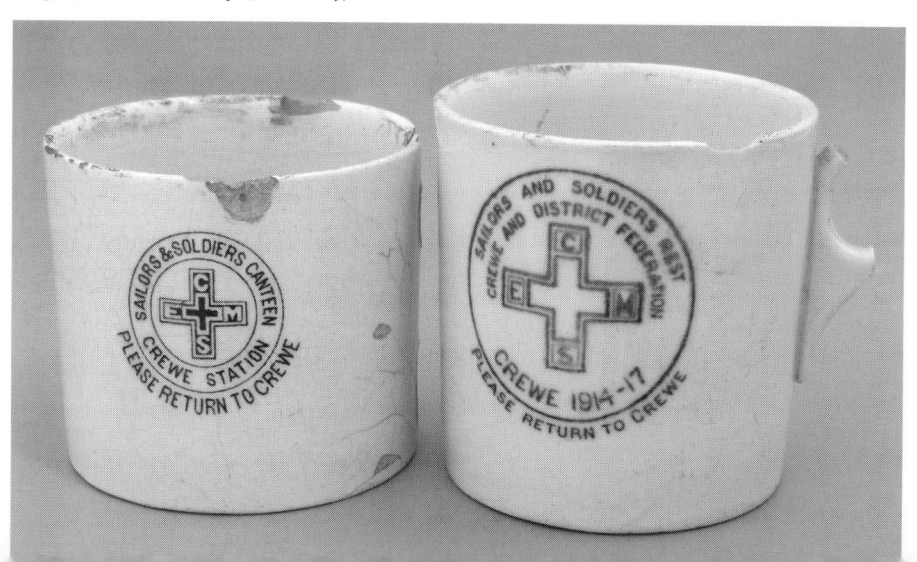

Interior of the Sailors' and Soldiers' Rest on Nantwich Road, which catered for around five hundred servicemen every week, some of whom would need a bed. *(Mary and Colin Maclean)*

the Ancre Heights. His luck was not to last however, for he was killed near St Quentin in the massive German offensive in the spring of 1918. Lance Corporal J. Austin (New Street), aged 19, received the same medal for working on a parapet in full view of the enemy on Christmas Eve 1916. Serving on HMS *Thrasher*, Gunner S Proudlove (Holland Street) won a DCM in February 1917. Crewe nurses also were receiving recognition for their work, with Sister E. Dodd (West Street) of the Territorial Nursing Service being decorated by the Red Cross, along with Sister E. Gibson. Another Crewe nurse who received local publicity was Miss Dorothy Snelson, the daughter of a foreman boiler maker. After serving six months in a military hospital, the ship she should have returned on was torpedoed. The distinguished service of Sister Ethel Lyon (Hungerford Road), of the Territorial Force Nurses, was recognized, though her brother, Lieutenant Claude Lyon, could not celebrate her achievement as he was killed in November 1916.

Other local victims of German submarines include Sapper L.G. Colclough (Mill Street), who was in the Mediterranean Sea for six hours before he was rescued after the ship he was on was sunk by a submarine on New Year's Day 1917. The boat in question, RMS *Ivernia*, was captained by William Turner, who had been in charge of the *Lusitania* when that was torpedoed in 1915. Four months later, Company Sergeant Major Joe Linnell (Gresty Road), serving with the RASC, was transferring to Alexandria via

Salonika, along with over a 1,000 other troops, when HM Transport *Acadian* was hit by a torpedo as it sailed the Agean Sea. Within six minutes the boat had sunk, though over a 1,000 men were rescued. Tragically, Joe Linnell was one of the 300 or so who were drowned, leaving a wife and three children.

An interesting letter from three Crewe men was published in the *Chronicle* describing the travails of 285 Battery RFA that was fighting the Turks:

'... we have travelled about 140 miles of desert ... we are nearly all fed up with seeing nothing but sand for months: last week we had a sand-storm which lasted for three days and we had nothing but sand for breakfast, dinner and tea. Now it is so hot we can hardly breathe ... it is just the opposite at night, when it goes very cold.'

A few weeks later, W.H. Eaton, of the Crewe Artillery Battery, added further colour:

'... our thirst was increased by the blast of the guns, for we had a flank and head wind most of the time. What with the blast and dust and heat our thirst was terrific ... our mouths had a nasty taste for a day or two after.'

Another Crewe man, Corporal F. Malam was wounded in his foot fighting the Turks in the Holy Land, a long way from his home in Goulden Street where he had been brought up and from the Grocery Department of Crewe Co-operative Society where he was formerly employed. A Crewe soldier who died fighting in another theatre of war, yet still in the glare of the eastern sun, was Private Noel Ankers, killed in action in April 1917 in Mesopotamia and whose name is recorded on the Basra War Memorial.

Other deaths occurred naturally in the town, away from military action. Dr James Atkinson, one of Crewe's most prominent men, breathed his last in March 1917. He was the Borough's first mayor, a County Councillor and one of LNWR's first Company doctors, eventually building Mirion House in Earle Street. That same month death also claimed Alderman Harry Hoptroff, a butcher of Market Street, who twice held the mayoral office. National events other than death caused Councillor John Williams to resign his seat in order to deputize as national organizer of the National Union of General Workers, in place of J.R. Clynes MP. He (Clynes) had been asked by Lloyd George to assist Lord Rhonda at the Ministry of Food, as the shortages were becoming critical, meaning that Williams was often away from Crewe on union work.

Owing to the shortages of food and coal and the general rise in prices, there was a national undercurrent of labour unrest. Three articles in the *Daily Mail* outlined the causes of the trouble, in which Crewe figured quite prominently. The question was posed as to why the town was prone to 'the influence of the extreme apostles of discontent, unrest and revolt.' James Tattersall, the Conservative agent for the Crewe division, blamed the ability of socialists to foment industrial disputes, even to citing the recently promoted union organizer John Williams as the main protagonist for peddling class myths that set the poor against the rich. Regardless of the perceived cause, the local papers were able to report the details of a short strike by the Amalgamated Society of Engineers complaining about dilution of labour, profiteering and price inflation not covered by wage rises.

At the same time, there was a tragic event that was widely covered in all the local papers, when a woman in Heath's Cottages (off Flag Lane) was accused of causing death through an illegal operation. It was of course an attempt by a working class woman to rid herself of an unwanted pregnancy by approaching a back-street abortionist. The dead lady, who was 34 and a mother of six, was employed at the chemical works at Lostock Gralam and did not want to lose her job, which was financing her son through the Grammar School at Northwich. After consulting a friend in Crewe, she went to Heath's Cottages, where eventually some form of instrument was used to terminate the pregnancy. The price was half a guinea, which would be returned if unsuccessful. The real price was a painful death for the expectant mother and three years penal servitude for the illegal abortionist.

Despite the serious war situation, with its remorseless demand upon the industrial resources of the country, the LNWR works in Crewe was virtually silent in the first week of July when the men had a much needed week's holiday. As one of the privileges of working for the Company was free travel; something between 9,000 and 10,000 passes were issued, to places such as Blackpool, London and the north Wales coast. It was possible that school teachers could not have afforded a holiday away from Crewe that year, as the war bonus awarded to them to cover rising prices was two shillings and not the ten shillings they had requested. One of the councillors suggested that they could always find a second job to make up their wages. At that juncture there were many adverts in the *Chronicle* for cooks, counter assistants and farm labourers, though under DORA regulations 'no person engaged on war work can live more than 10 miles away from his employment.'

In Russia one of the momentous events of the twentieth century occurred and one of its effects locally was a resolution passed by the Crewe Labour Party 'congratulating the Russian people in their glorious achievement of liberty', while at the same time welcoming the definite statement of war aims from the provincial government. A couple of weeks later there was a similar resolution from Crewe Trades Council acknowledging the war aim statement that 'removes all lust for conquest and imperialistic gain.' War aims were a lively topic, at national as well as local level, especially after the formation of the National War Aims Committee (NWAC) in 1917. It was around this time that Siegfried Sassoon famously threw the ribbon of his Military Cross into the Mersey and had his letter of defiance read out in Parliament because he, too, was dissatisfied with the lack of clarity over war aims.

By the late summer of 1917 the NAWC had held meetings in Willaston, Malkins Bank, Shavington, Wheelock, Haslington, Mow Cop, Alsager and twice in Crewe. A third meeting was arranged in Crewe Town Hall, when Ernest Craig, Joseph Davies and Bowen Cooke made speeches to counter 'the undermining and deceitful German ideas that were being disseminated up and down Crewe and throughout the country.' According to the speakers, it would be better in this 'war to end all wars' to be dead rather than fall into the hands of the Germans. War aims, expressed by the NAWC and its acolytes, included making restitution to Belgium, the whole cost of the war repaid to the allies by the Central Powers and the restoration of the Ten Commandments in Germany, with a binding undertaking to carry them out. The latter point was never raised at the Peace Conference at Versailles.

A Crewe man, who regularly seemed to provoke anything but peaceful feelings amongst some in the town, was Withoff, the pork butcher that we first met in Chapter One. In May 1917, he (Withoff) claimed in court that Arthur Cooke, a butcher of Mill Street, had assaulted him at an auction sale after insulting him at various times over the past months. In his defence Cooke complained that on Withoff's father's grave was the inscription 'sacred to the memory', even though he was born in Prussia. This, according to Cooke, was treason. On being advised by the court to apologize, Cooke claimed he would never apologize to a German. Eventually he did, along with paying a fine of three pounds.

Fines were also levied against many Crewe people later in the year, for wrongfully acquiring sugar for preserving domestic fruit and jam making. The regulations prohibited extra sugar if the fruit was purchased, rather than self-grown, a regulation ignored by over fifty householders, meaning an average fine of £4, including costs. A couple of weeks later, further prosecutions of thirty-four persons brought another £172-5-0 in fines. Some of the culprits expressed their dismay at the travesty of rural dwellers growing fruit in their large gardens, who could purchase sugar with impunity, while Crewe housewives who bought the fruit were grabbed by the law when they attempted to make jam.

The sacrifice of so many men is presented to succeeding generations by organized school visits to the battlefields of northern France and Belgium. Here, Thomas Flude of Shavington High School is pointing out the name of his great uncle on the Menin Gate. *(Dorothy Flude)*

One of the architectural features of the present face of the town was unveiled, in the summer of 1917, when the Marquis of Crewe opened the Prudential Buildings, on the corner of Market Street and Chester Street. Any new building was unusual in wartime Crewe, a situation that caused the closure of the Britannia Brick Works in McLaren Street, until the war ended, when demand for bricks allowed its reopening for a decade or so. No doubt the powerful financial muscle of the Prudential enabled the scheme to be successfully completed, though by non-Crewe labour it must be said. On Friday 24 August, the great and good of the town assembled for a conducted tour by the local executive of the Prudential who, tragically, was to lose both of his pilot officer sons before the end of November. These offices still remain as an attractive feature in the centre of the town. If the ceremony had been arranged a couple of weeks

1917 ANOTHER YEAR OF SACRIFICE

earlier it could have been combined with a meeting on the Square to mark the third anniversary of the war, when wounded servicemen and relatives of the slain gathered with the mayor and other dignitaries to commemorate the commencement of hostilities.

About eight months after the start of the war a Sailors' and Soldiers' Rest Room had been established on Nantwich Road, in the former Railway Mission Room, about a hundred yards from the railway station, enabling servicemen to have meals or even a bed for the night. The weekly takings were around £300, which helped to pay for 18,700 pies, 500 lb of tea, 700 lb of sugar and 840 pints of milk. Towards the end of 1917, the Church of England Men's Society, responsible for this much used room, decided to commence a canteen service on the station for soldiers travelling through Crewe. Three hundred women volunteered to service the tea-trolleys, supplied by the LNWR. Special crockery was manufactured with the name of the organization and the instructions 'Return to Crewe'.

In August there occurred at Whiston's picture frame makers in Mill Street (one of over 300 workshops in Crewe) a dreadful though not uncommon accident when a 15-year-old employee died as a result of her clothing catching fire. Open fires were the rule in homes and small factories, which brought injury and death, especially to young children. A few weeks before this, Private Tom Marriott (Lockett Street) of the 2nd Battalion Manchester Regiment suffered a similar fate when he was caught in the blast of liquid fire from a German flame-thrower in Belgium, a hideous way of death and destruction introduced by the Germans in 1915.

In the summer of 1917 began another battle that ranks alongside the Somme for a long, hard, military slog, with very little obvious strategic benefit. This was the Third Battle of Ypres or as it is better known, Passchendaele. Needless to say, the local papers devoted columns to the struggle and the Crewe men who perished there. Sergeant S.L. Dunn (Alexandra Street), aged 19, won the Military Medal for gallant conduct at Messines Ridge

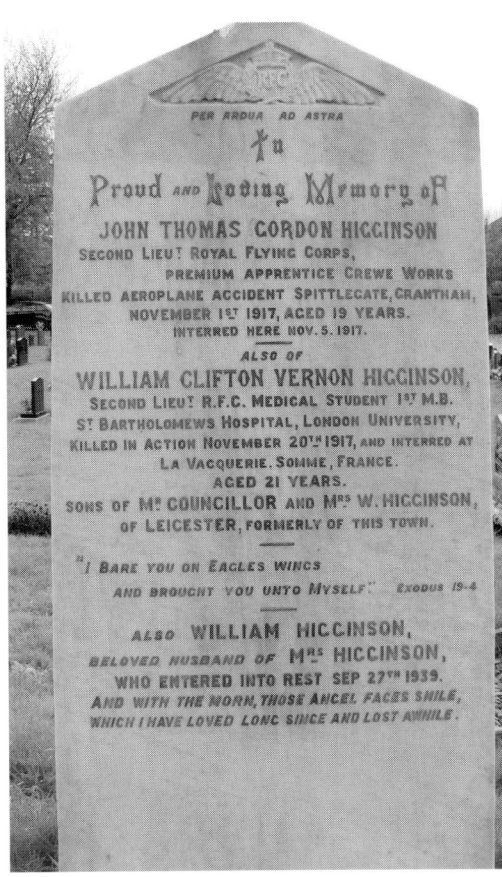

The details on this grave marker are a stark reminder that war can wipe out several family members in a matter of days. The Royal Flying Corps attracted many of the better educated young men, such as these two brothers from Crewe who both had promising careers.

Second from the right is Harry Holdcroft (Underwood Lane), a fitter in the LNWR Erecting Shop, who went all through the war with the Crewe Artillery Battery. Despite the horrific scenes he witnessed he never lost his Christian faith.

at the start of the campaign, only to be shot on the 2 August while attempting to bayonet three of the enemy. Corporal William Hodkinson (Underwood Lane), previously a timekeeper with the LNWR, was killed the same day that Captain H.P. Beames was marking the third anniversary of 'this righteous war' at the meeting on the Square. He has no known grave; his memorial is a name engraved on the Menin Gate. Another Crewe man, whose name is on the same memorial, was Private John H. Tudor who, after being wounded at Loos and the Somme, was killed in action on 11 August, attacking Westhoek Ridge with the 10th Cheshires. Private Walter Coleman's mother (Fleet Street) received news of her son's death on 8 August which, according to the mayor, was Mother's Day. He had been fighting with the King's Liverpool Regiment during the Third Battle of Ypres.

Casualty notifications were also now arriving in the town from a new source as the Royal Flying Corps expanded. August 1917 saw the end of a promising career as a concert violinist, when Second Lieutenant Frank Tipping (Nantwich Road), a member

Nantwich Road looking west. The psychical photographer, William Hope, had his premises just east of the shops and eating house. The Royal Hotel (home of Lieutenant Alan Welch, who won the Military Cross) can be seen on the north side of Nantwich Road.
(Mary and Colin Maclean)

of the Hallé Orchestra whom the *Manchester Guardian* described as 'most brilliant', crashed in France. Another resident of Nantwich Road, Second Lieutenant Gerald Pearson, aged 19, had been called back to France after two days leave. A former scholar of Sandbach School, he also crashed his aeroplane after only a few days with his squadron.

By November the campaign in Palestine, which included the Crewe Battery of Artillery, was being successfully concluded, for on 9 December Jerusalem had been taken from the Turks. Harry Holdcroft, (Underwood Lane), a LNWR fitter, who had joined up in August 1914 and who became a preacher with the Christian Brethren, often spoke of celebrating Christmas in Jerusalem. Another Crewe man, Private Walter Smith (Edleston Road), serving in Palestine with the Cheshires, won the Military Medal, whereas Gunner Walter Gladden, also fighting in the east, was severely gassed in July. He survived the war to become a teacher at the Higher Elementary School in Brierley Street, in addition to writing articles for the *Manchester Guardian*. It might interest some to know that he was the first editor of the Secondary School's magazine *The Gridiron*, as well as the author of *Cheshire Folk*.

The end of 1917 in Crewe was marked by the death of William McNeill, who had been concerned in civic affairs for around sixty years. A doyen of the Liberal Party, he

A view of Tyne Cot Military Cemetery which contains nearly 12,000 war graves, near to the village of Passchendaele. At least twenty-five Crewe men are remembered here, including Private J.T. Jobson of the Royal Warwickshire Regiment, who was killed in action on 3 September 1917. He previously lived in Buxton Avenue and worked for W.H. Smith (newsagents) overlooking the Square.

was also a staunch Primitive Methodist and five times mayor. Another man who breathed his last, with less people to mourn his passing, was Jonas Potts, who Professor Chaloner, the town's premier historian, termed Crewe's chief jerry builder. He certainly made a lot of money out of building houses, leaving an estate worth over £30,000. And so another year ended with severe shortages and industrial unrest appearing, yet without any sign of victory in a war that was supposedly only going to last until Christmas 1914.

Chapter Five

1918 Enduring to Victory

'We are now entering that period of the war when the strain will be most severely felt and the powers of endurance of every member of the community will be tested.' *Winston Churchill in a letter to the Crewe Brotherhood, January 1918*

THE FIRST WEEK of 1918 saw every seat in the Kino Picture House sold out for every performance, with hundreds more wanting seats just to see Charlie Chaplin in his sixth film, *The Pawn Shop*, which had been released three months previously. Alternative entertainment was provided by *Cinderella* at the theatre, or the ladies of the munitions department of the LNWR Works playing football for charity, raising £57, which was divided between the Cottage Hospital and the Red Cross. Entertainment was also utilized for propaganda purposes. This was arranged by the War Aims Committee, in April, when a giant screen was hung in front of the three storey Market Terrace dwellings to show scenes of the Zeppelin bomb damage in London, along with images of action in the Holy Land, France, tanks, trench warfare and naval engagements. Hundreds turned out to watch and to listen to Major T. Barnshaw informing them of the present state of hostilities.

If the authorities ever had any qualms about diminishing patriotism or lack of

Wartime parades and demonstrations were often held on the Square, though this image is from 1912. The Square was given to the town by the LNWR Company in 1893.

confidence in the eventual triumph of the Allied cause, they only needed to glance at the amount of war savings invested by the people of Crewe. Second only to the volunteering of persons was the willing volunteering of wealth by the working class of Crewe. In the last three months of 1917 some £32,000 was invested in war bonds at 5 per cent interest per annum. Six months later, that had risen to £609,000. This is the true index of their patriotism, despite the grumbling undertones of some newspapers, which stated that the men of Crewe were being disloyal when they took industrial action to preserve, or even enhance, their pay.

Acute food shortages that had disfigured the last weeks of 1917 continued into the New Year to such an extent that children were kept away from school to reserve a place in the ever lengthening queues that began as early as 3.30 am. The major cause was not only the lack of food; rather what did exist was bought and hoarded by the more affluent. As the food queues grew longer and more numerous, so tempers flared, causing so much trouble that the police had to be called, meaning some erstwhile shoppers had to appear before the magistrates charged with a breach of the peace. Eventually the government realized that the only answer was some form of rationing.

Crewe Borough Food Control Committee submitted a rationing plan, worked out by Feltham, the Town Clerk, to the Area Food Controller for his approval. Each household had to register with a local butcher and grocer for meat, tea, margarine and butter, which were the only items then rationed. Some 10,500 ration cards were delivered by eighty teachers to Crewe homes, entitling each recipient to one quarter pound of margarine and half a pound of meat. By the beginning of February Feltham's scheme, which had been accepted by the Food Controllers of Congleton, Sandbach, Alsager, Malpas and Nantwich, worked sufficiently well that food queues all but disappeared across south Cheshire.

Later in the year, coal was so short that it, too, was rationed, despite efforts at

Tune commemorating a local war death composed by Joseph Stubbs of the Music Warehouse in Mill Street. Stubbs was the organist and choirmaster at the Primitive Methodist Church in Mill Street.

equalizing supply and prices via the Retail Coal Price Order of 1917. Under this Order, fourteen Crewe coal merchants set a price that was seven shillings and sixpence above 1914 prices. By the end of 1917, coal had risen by another 25 per cent. Six months later coal supplies were dwindling even further, meaning that the council enforced a regulation prohibiting anyone purchasing more than one month's supply. Two months before the war ended, a full blown scheme came into operation, whereby each householder had to register with a coal-merchant, so that they could be sure of their allocation of fuel.

As we saw in the last chapter, Defence of the Realm Regulations demanded that no one could live more than 10 miles away from their place of employment if engaged on munitions or other war work. Another Order that impinged upon the reading households of the town was the rationing of paper, meaning that the sizes of all the local newspapers had to be reduced and only sold to regular orders with no copies left for casual sales. Even when the tide of war was turning in favour of the Allies in October there were still people prosecuted for lighting offences being told that 'the war was not over.' Chip shops were not allowed to fry after 9.00 pm, as Nellie Proctor of Victoria Street found to her cost, when she was fined five shillings for selling chips at 10.45 pm.

War conditions also affected the liquor trade for, as we have noted, the hours of opening had been altered as had the specific gravity of beer. This meant that court

The Co-operative Society's new bakery, opened in 1916 in Baker Street, was one of the few buildings erected during the war years.

proceedings against drunkenness had declined from eighty-five in 1913 to thirty in just four years. By February 1918, pub landlords were discussing a form of rationing, as they regularly ran short of beer. Consequently, in April, a conference of the Lancashire and Cheshire Licensed Victuallers' Association was held at Crewe seeking a solution for the problem. A voluntary scheme was introduced whereby spirits would not be sold in larger measures than a glass, and only half pints of draught beer could be ordered. Outdoor supplies were proportionally restricted, with beer and spirits not to be served together and, finally, supplies to be divided into seven equal portions to cover each opening period.

Another aspect of domestic life affected by the war, that took many years to be even partially rectified, was that of housing. Crewe contained just over 9000 houses that were said to be suitable for the working class which, according to the council's figures, left a shortfall of about 500 dwellings. Purchasing a house did not automatically mean that the buyer could live in it. There are many cases where the sitting tenant would not move because no dwellings were available to accommodate him. Virtually all building had been suspended for the duration of hostilities, which resulted in house sharing, to the extent that 440 houses each contained two families. The last plans for a new dwelling house were submitted to the appropriate Council committee in May 1916. Only ten applications were made for building alterations between August 1916 and December 1918, meaning that for most of the last two years of war the Council works' committee did not include planning items on their agenda.

As the numbers of soldiers discharged from the services increased, owing to wounds and injuries, measures were taken to ease their transition back into society. In February, Cheshire Education Committee was advertising for an instructor in commercial subjects to instruct disabled soldiers and sailors. Classes were held in Crewe to teach them the rudiments of repairing petrol engines, or attending to tractors, for which they received £4-0-0 a week while under tuition. The Council of the Mechanics' Institution allowed their facilities to be used for training twenty men under the auspices of a Soldiers' and Sailors' Society. This latter movement, the National Federation of Discharged and Demobilized Soldiers and Sailors, had a branch in the town by the end of 1917, with an office above 71 Victoria Street.

Details of the wounded were regularly recorded in the columns of the local papers, so we know that Private H. Silvester (Ruskin Road), who volunteered at 17, was wounded at the Somme, drafted to Egypt before being rescued from the sea after his boat was torpedoed, only to lose his left arm at the Battle of Gaza. Rifleman William Tomkinson, whose trade was boot repairing, lost his right arm at the age of 20. Private L. Evans (Earle Street), was in hospital with frost damaged feet, while Private Reginald Dutton (Nile Street) was being treated for his injuries in a German hospital as a prisoner.

Awards were still being won, even in this quiet period of the war. Lieutenant Alan Welch (Royal Hotel), who had been serving since 1914, received a Military Cross for distinguished service. Two other Crewe men, who won the Military Medal, were Private Norman Conde (Lewis Street), of the Royal Welsh Fusiliers and Private Jack Edwards (Catherine Street), serving with the East Surrey Regiment, at the Battle of Cambrai. He (Edwards) had twice filtered through enemy lines with dispatches. Lieutenant Cyril

Name.	Address.	Regiment Joined.	Name.	Address.	Regiment Joined.
ARROW, AMOS	195, Market Street, Crewe	Cheshires.	FARRELL, GEORGE A.	16, Church Street, Crewe	A.O.C.
(Died of wounds received in action, Jan. 19, 1918)			FROST, THOMAS	23, Liverpool Street, Crewe	3/7th Cheshires.
HESHIRE, WILLIAM L.	14, Bedford Street, Crewe	K.L.R.	FARR, F. (Committee)	11, Stoneley Road, Crewe	R.E.
(Died)			FINCH, JAMES HENRY	23, Stamford Avenue, Crewe	R.F.C.
UTTON, ERNEST G.	12, St. Clair Street, Crewe	17th Cheshires.	FINCH, WM. HICKSON	120, Alton Street, Crewe	R.G.A.
(Killed in action)			GAWTHORNE, CLIFFORD	Mill Street, Crewe	A.S.C.
ATT, EDWIN	26, Coppice Road, Willaston	Royal Engineers.	GLENN, OLIVER	62, Mill Street, Crewe	R.F.A.
REECE, HERBERT H.	285, Alton Street, Crewe	3rd Cheshires.	(w) GROCOTT, JOSEPH	84, Alton Street, Crewe	Manchester Pals.
(Killed in action)			GORDON, WILLIAM	72, Queen Street, Crewe	Manchester Pals.
AKESHAFT, PERCY	1, Ridgway Street, Crewe	5th Cheshires.	GRIFFIES, BERT	5, Railway Street, Crewe	R.A.M.C.
ALLWOOD, AMBROSE	7, Mellor Street, Crewe	King's Royal Rifles.	GOODWIN, PERCY	20, Harding Street, Crewe	Motor Transport.
(Died of wounds)			GUEST, HENRY	72, Oakley Street, Crewe	3rd Cheshires.
EST, ARTHUR	373, West Street, Crewe	14th Cheshires.	GREENWOOD, JOSEPH HY.	30, Stoneley Road, Crewe	3/7th Cheshires.
(Killed in action)			GORDON, CHARLES FREDERICK.	72, Queen Street, Crewe	R.G.A.
			GRESTY, JAMES	Osborne Grove, Shavington	3rd Cheshires.
REWS, HARRY	121, Bradfield Road, Crewe	A.S.C.	HUMPHRIES, HAROLD	62, Westminster Street, Crewe	R.F.A.
MAN, ALBERT	15, Chell Street, Crewe	R.F.A.	HUMPHRIES, THOS. SAML. G.	8, Stoneley Road, Crewe	2/5 Yorkshires.
ERS, ERNEST	77, Samuel Street, Crewe	A.O.C.	(w) HOWES, REGINALD	42, Westminster Street, Crewe	Liverpool Pals.
LEY, EDWARD	196, Alton Street, Crewe	R.G.A.	(w) HORNSEY, HARRY	64, Selfton Avenue, Crewe	Liverpool Pals.
WOOD, DAVID	9, Middlewich Street, Crewe	R.G.A.	HASSALL, HORACE	Alston Bldgs, Barony, N'wich	A.S.C.
			(w) HOLLINS, WALTER E.	26, Ridgway Street, Crewe	7th Cheshire Territorials.
ALL, JOHN	67, West Street, Crewe	Cheshires.	HILL, CHARLES	19, Sheppard Street, Crewe	Shropshire L. Infantry.
HELL, JOHN K.	78, Samuel Street, Crewe	3rd Cheshires.	HILL, ALBERT EDWARD	79, Ridgway Street, Crewe	R.G.A.
FEY, FREDERICK	115, Market Street, Crewe	R.A.M.C.	HOUGH, HARRY	261, Alton Street, Crewe	A.S.C.
OLEY, ARTHUR	18, Liverpool Terrace, Crewe	7th Cheshire Territorials.	HODSON, ARNOLD	50, Ludford Street, Crewe	Cheshires.
TERS, THOMAS	120, Bedford Street, Crewe	A.S.C.	*HISSEY, JAMES WILLIAM	30, Derrington Street, Crewe	R.G.A.
GESS, GEORGE	71, Beech Street, Crewe	Motor Transport.	HEWITT, ARNOLD	79, Richard Moon Street, Crewe	R.A.M.C.
NET, STANLEY M.	Haslington, near Crewe	R.G.A.	HULME, WILLIAM B.	35, Henry Street, Crewe	A.O.C.
WN, CLEMENT	21, Vincent Street, Crewe	A.S.C.	HAYNES, JOHN WILLIAM	5, Delamere Street, W., Crewe	2/6th Cheshires.
WN, WM. CHAS.	16, Hungerford Avenue, Crewe	R.G.A.	HICKTON, FRANK M.	8, Bedford Street, Crewe	2/8th Lancs. Fusiliers.
IS, WM.	42, Middlewich Street, Crewe	R.E.	HOUGH, H. M.	16, Westminster Street, Crewe	R.F.A.
HAN, HAROLD	17, Hungerford Terrace, Crewe	R.A.R.E.	HOWARTH, BENJAMIN HAIGH.	2, Stalbridge Road, Crewe	R.F.A.
ES, SAMUEL	78, Stewart Street, Crewe	R.G.A.	*HODGKINSON, J. L.		
KER, WM. H.	63, Thomas Street, Crewe	17th Cheshires.	JACKSON, JOSEPH	Richard Moon Street, Crewe	3/7th Cheshires.
TERS, GEORGE H.	91, Westminster Street, Crewe	2/5th R.W.F.	*(w)JENNINGS, JOHN H.	48, Remer Street, Crewe	Cheshires.
TER, REGINALD	157, Walthall Street, Crewe		JENKINS, HORACE	36, Manchester Street, Crewe	R.F.A.
WN, LEONARD	4, Underwood Lane, Crewe	75th Training Reserve Batt.	JONES, LUTHER	15, Mellor Street, Crewe	Welsh Fusiliers.
RON, ARTHUR	77, Westminster Street, Crewe	R.E.	JONES, WILLIAM THOMAS	171, Wistaston Road, Crewe	R.A.M.C.
CE, WALTER	27, Bedford Street, Crewe	Manchester Pals.	JOHNSON, THOMAS WILLIAM	5, Culland Street, Crewe	King's Royal Rifles.
STERS, JOHN	75, Alexandra Street, Crewe	R.F.A.	JONES, FRANK	Haslington, near Crewe	Shropshire L. Infantry.
RKE, HERBERT JOHN	23, Marsh Lane, Nantwich	R.F.A.	JONES, FRANCIS WILLIAM	201 Walthall Street, Crewe	R.F.A.
SWELL, WALTER R.	58, Samuel Street, Crewe	10th Middlesex.	JONES, HARRY	16, Bridle Road, Crewe	4th Cheshires.
PER, FRANK	23, Derrington Avenue, Crewe	R.A.M.C.	JONES, ERNEST	220, Hungerford Road, Crewe	50th Training Reserve Batt.
PER, CECIL E.	131, Mill Street, Crewe	2/7 Lancs. Fusiliers.			
PER, CECIL E.	397, West Street, Crewe	R.A.M.C.	KINSEY, GEORGE	18, Newdigate Street, Crewe	A.S.C.
UGH, SYDNEY	14, Victoria Street, Crewe	R.A.M.C.	KINSEY, FREDERICK	18, Newdigate Street, Crewe	A.S.C.
KE, JOHN	54, Sheppard Street, Crewe	A.S.C.	KEELEY, THOMAS	58, Sheppard Street, Crewe	R.F.A.
KE, ARTHUR	54, Sheppard Street, Crewe	7th Cheshires.			
NES, JOHN	6, Coronation Street, Crewe	Royal Engineers.	LLOYD, STEPHEN	6, Sheppard Street, Crewe	R.F.A.
TTERTON, FREDERICK	240, Walthall Street, Crewe	R.F.C.	LEEDHAM, ERNEST	Osborne Grove, Shavington	Cheshire Imp. Yeomanry.
TERILL, JOHN	75, Victoria Street, Crewe		LEECH, HARRY	98, Nelson Street, Crewe	R.G.A.
			LEIGHTON, WM. E.	34, Derrington Street, Crewe	Shropshire L. Infantry.
BYSHIRE, ALFRED	56, Lockett Street, Crewe	A.S.C.	LATHAM, JAMES	Wistaston, near Crewe	R.A.R.E.
AN, HARRY	56, Chetwode Street, Crewe	Welsh Fusiliers.	LOWE, ALFRED	456, Underwood Lane, Crewe	R.A.R.E.
TON, FRANK L.	181, Walthall Street, Crewe	3rd Cheshires.	LATHAM, THOMAS	4, Coronation Street, Crewe	South Lancashires.
IES, TREVOR	18, Buxton Avenue, Crewe	R.N.V.R.	LOCKETT, HARRY M.	74, Stewart Street, Crewe	R.G.A.
D, W. J.	142, Wistaston Road, Willaston	4th Cheshires.	LITTLER, JOSEPH WILSON	174, Wistaston Road, Crewe	2/9th Manchesters.
			LLOYD, WILLIAM G.	145, Westminster Street, Crewe	R.G.A.
NSON, SIDNEY	69, Hungerford Road, Crewe	A.S.C.	LATHAM, GEORGE WILLIAM	44, Buxton Avenue, Crewe	R.N.V.R.
			LEEK, THOS. SAML.	163, Walthall Street, Crewe	Motor Transport.

* Discharged from the Colours and re-instated in the employment of the Society. (v) Prisoner. (w) Wounded in action.

Crewe Co-operative Society published, in their quarterly report, the names of all employees who had joined the colours. This is one page from the 286th report, dated March 1917.

McHale (Sefton Avenue), aged 28, won his Military Cross on New Year's Day while serving with the South Lancashire Regiment. He became the first CO of the 7th Cheshire Battalion of the Home Guard during the Second World War.

Amongst the seven Crewe men killed in the desultory fighting during the first two months of 1918 were Sapper Arthur Venables, killed in action on 7 February and Private Herbert Walters (Brown Street), fighting with the South Lancashire Regiment, killed on 25 January. Private Thomas Wolbrom (Broad Street), aged 20, died five days into 1918 from wounds received a couple of days earlier. His name is recorded on the Memorial at Tyne Cot Military Cemetery, he having no known grave. Another man who died at this time was Captain George Dodd, Marine Superintendent of the Cunard Line, whose ship was torpedoed while on government contract work. Five years previously his brother, Edward, a junior engineer on the *Titanic*, went down with that ship. Their father still lived in the family home in West Street, along with their sister who, as we learned in the last chapter, received an award for her nursing services in France.

At the end of February a leader in the *Crewe Guardian* speculated that the whispers coming from the western front meant that a big attack was in the offing. At the end of March all the portents exploded in a clash of arms, as the Germans made a massive attack across a 50 mile front, assisted by troops transferred from the east where the Russian Revolution had ended that country's participation in the war. Popularly known as the Kaiser's Battle, this spring offensive was one of the greatest battles in the four year struggle on the western front. This is not the place to detail the tactics that led to massive gains of territory and capture of prisoners, but yet still did not lead to the collapse of the British Third and Fifth armies. What this fighting did achieve was to add more unwanted names to the 'roll of honour' columns in the local papers.

The 11th Cheshires was part of the 25th Division holding a position near Chaufours Wood, east of Beugnatre, where Sergeant Major Herbert Farrington, who had won a Military Medal about fifteen months previously, was killed by shell fire on 22 March on the second day of the battle. Having no known grave, his name is engraved on the Arras Memorial. His young son later worked at Crewe Rolls-Royce. Second Lieutenant Joseph Bostock (Hungerford Road), also of the Cheshire Regiment, was killed in action two days after Herbert Farrington. He was a teacher at Bedford Street and had only been married for three months. Corporal Harold Glover (next door neighbour to the Villiers Russell twins before the war), enlisted in September 1914, only to fall in the fighting of 21 March. He had been awarded the Military Medal in 1917. Private John Wallis Ranicar (formerly Accounts Office, Crewe Co-operative Society) of the Royal Welsh Fusiliers, was killed on 22 April. His father had been drowned whilst skating on Betley Mere when John was a babe in arms. His second name 'Wallis' is derived from his grandfather, George Wallis, who gave his name to Wallis Street in Crewe. Another man killed in this battle was Albert Lockett, son of a shoe-maker, with premises in Earle Street. When the March Offensive began Lockett was on leave with his wife Alice. He was killed shortly after returning to the front with the King's Liverpool Regiment. Like many war widows, Alice remarried when the war was over. All told, nearly forty Crewe men were killed in March and April 1918.

Many more were injured, such as Second Lieutenant W. H. Struthers, son of Crewe's Director of Education, who was shot in the shoulder; Gunner Alfred Stubbs (Lunt Avenue) of the Royal Garrison Artillery (RGA), an insurance agent in civvy street, was wounded for the third time; whereas Corporal Rowland Dentith of the King's Liverpool, who was wounded on 28 April, died next day at a casualty clearing station. Private Harold Strawport (Swinnerton Street), who worked for Crewe Co-op before he enlisted, was wounded and captured by the Germans and treated in a German hospital. Private A.H. Dean (Bank Street) was hit in the face while fighting with the Cheshires. Private A. Lupton was injured by a bullet hitting his wrist, making it highly probable he never went back to his former job as a blacksmith's striker in the Old Works.

Urgent pleas for reinforcements were received from the military authorities in France, pleas which caused a fresh examination of exempted men. The workforce at the LNWR works was combed once more and yielded another 400 young men. This caused a further backlash of complaints that the rural areas were not supplying their share, with the sons of farmers being identified as the main 'slackers'. Consequently, many certificates of exemption were withdrawn from men working in agriculture so that they could be resubmitted to the tribunals. In their defence, however, it must be pointed out as Lyn MacDonald in *To the Last Man* writes:

'When food stocks grew dangerously low, 2,000 skilled ploughmen were winkled out of the Army and returned to the land.'

The winter of 1917/18 marked a time when food stocks were at a dangerously low level.

The shortage of recruits exercised the minds of the officials at Whitehall for, as the *Crewe Chronicle* reported, men between 42 and 44 were now considered for conscription under the latest Military Service Regulations, with a suggestion from the Director of National Service and Lloyd George that men up to 50-years-old could be conscripted for non-military duties. An advertisement also appeared for volunteers for Queen Mary's Army Auxiliary Corps, so that women could replace the men called up. Thirty thousand ladies were required nationally for clerical and domestic work. A Land Army recruiting rally was held in Crewe in June to gain further offers of help from interested ladies. As this rally consisted of a procession of hay wagons, horses, land-girls carrying rakes and spades, dairy maids and Girl Guides, all preceded by a Boy Scouts' band, it certainly proved a success as a free public spectacle.

Not all of the enlisted men were at the cutting edge of the fight, whether against Germans or other forces of the Central Powers. In an anonymous diary of a battalion's transport officer, serving in Mesopotamia (probably kept by a south Cheshire man), the following entry was made for 6 April 1918, when a desperate slogging match was being fought in France:

'Big show and horse racing at Basra. All of my cars out carrying passengers. Expect a few accidents … . Go off to the races with a few of my pals. Glorious sights. All the Arabs and high people of the place mixing with brigadiers, generals and ladies of the Harem on the Grand Stand. Marvellous sights in the paddock. Back a few horses but poor prices. Sun very hot. Races again next day.'

Not all warfare was drudgery, boredom and terror, as can be seen from this image where two members of the Mesopotamia Expeditionary Force (wireless section) enjoy a game of tennis in Baghdad in May 1918.

There are other entries that detail incidents when they were close to the Turks and even a description of the scene where General Townshend surrendered at Kut. Perhaps the last entry for the beginning of September redresses the balance:

> 'Have just been to see some of my boys who are in the field hospital. Its wicked to see how they have faded away.'

Whether in France, Persia, Palestine, Greece, Italy or East Africa war meant suffering and boredom for most of the soldiers.

The annual scourge of influenza reappeared in Crewe in the winter of 1917/1918, with cases rising from 125 in December to 156 in February, the peak month. A chemist in the town advertised an immediate and complete cure for Spanish influenza at a shilling a bottle. Notwithstanding this miracle potion, the schools at Edleston Road and Pedley Street still had to be closed to prevent the spread of infection. Later in the year, Mill Street Wesleyan School was visited by George Charnock, an old pupil who had migrated from Crewe with his parents to the USA in 1884. Dressed in the uniform of an American serviceman, he must have been one of the first visible links of their new ally in the struggle with the Central Powers. A further point of interest is that Charnock's father was responsible for the introduction into the UK from America of Christian Endeavour, a very popular movement in nonconformist churches during the first half of the twentieth century, with Hightown Congregational Church, Crewe, being the first branch in the UK.

Faint foreshadows of an embryonic British Legion could be perceived in a letter to the *Chronicle*, published in July 1917, requesting a Soldiers' Association at the conclusion of the war. As it happened, such organizations appeared before the end of 1917, when a branch of the Discharged Soldiers' and Sailors' Association was commenced in the town, which by the summer of 1918 had around fifty members. We have already noted that another similar body was commenced when the National Federation of Discharged & Demobilized Soldiers and Sailors opened a branch office above 71 Victoria Street. In September a flag day was held for this latter Federation, which was trying to raise sufficient capital to purchase premises for recreational purposes.

In a speech reported in both the *Guardian* and the *Chronicle*, it was claimed that the Federation would remain separate from the Association as the latter had entered into the political arena by deciding to run parliamentary candidates. Consequently, when the vacant Liberal Unionist Club, in Edleston Road, was opened by the Federation, its use was strictly limited to its 220 members. This exclusiveness was continued after the war, for we find that in August 1919 the Federation arranged for widows and servicemen to be taken on an outing to Rhyl, whereas the Association took its members for a picnic at Llangollen. Eventually sanity prevailed, for by the end of 1919 the Federation and the Association co-operated with bodies such as the Crewe Comrades of the Great War and the LNWR Employees Committee, to form a common benevolent fund to assist ex-servicemen and their dependents.

While the German offensives were raging in the spring of 1918, which the *Crewe Guardian* called 'the mightiest battle the world has ever experienced', a unique fund raising event was held on the Square. This was the visit of a tank with the instruction 'Your duty

In May 1918 Crewe was visited by Drake, one of six tanks engaged on raising war savings. The scheme was a roaring success, raising over £150 million nationwide.
(Mary and Colin Maclean)

is to help pay for the War. Go to the tank and bank.' With the amount of blood and treasure that Crewe had expended upon the conflict, this slogan was patronising to say the least. As usual the great and the good stood in turn on the top of the tank (named Drake) to urge the crowd to give. By the end of the week over £509,000 had been raised, a similar amount to St Helens and Wigan; but a lot less than Rochdale managed. Of the Crewe total, £300,000 was invested by the LNWR; Greenall Whitley and Crewe Coop £5,000 each and Pat Collins, the local fairground operator, £2,000. Any resident with no capital could have availed himself of the Prudential's offer of a loan to be repaid over seven years.

Travelling shows continued to visit the towns and communities of England to bring a little light relief to all who had the time and money to attend. In May, Bronco Bill's Wild West Show and Mammoth Circus arrived in Crewe to set up its Big Top on spare ground in Flag Lane that was often used for such activities. With accommodation for 5000, and seats priced between one shilling (5p) and four shillings (20p), there was ample opportunity for families to be engrossed by the many acts and forget for a little while rationing and the disturbing news from France. Two concerts that were not allowed to proceed had been arranged by E.R. Foden of Nantwich Road to raise funds for the Soldiers' Rest and Canteen work. The rules of the Church of England Men's Society prohibited fund raising on Sundays, which was the day booked for a concert by Foden's Works Band.

A group of female munition workers who, according to G.R.S. Darroch, proved their worth manufacturing armaments in the LNWR Works, photographed outside the General Offices in 1918. Their participation in war work caused a radical change to the status of women, though when the war ended most of the ladies in this image were discharged from the Works. *(Mary and Colin Maclean)*

Every week there were showings of films at the Palace, the Empire or the Kino, in addition to live entertainment at the theatre in Heath Street. Regular competitive cricket continued in the quaintly named North Staffs and Crewe War Workers' League, as did football in the Cottage Hospital Cup and other competitions. Every week there would be events organized by charities and churches for those with time to participate. Some, however, offended the law when they visited fortune-tellers, meaning that four would-be female prophets were fined forty shillings or one month in gaol.

As the calendar reached the fourth anniversary of the war, muted celebrations marked the day, with the major event being a service in Christ Church. In front of the mayor and corporation, the Reverend Walter Bidlake gave a short address, after which the local dignitaries processed the few yards to the Municipal Buildings for more speeches. Half a mile away at St Paul's, on Hightown, a further service marked the beginning of hostilities, attended by the Crewe Volunteers and a large congregation. Not to be outdone, the Brotherhood also celebrated the occasion with the Union Flag and the Stars and Stripes draped across the Congregational church pulpit, where George Charnock, the ex-Crewe man, was the speaker.

Four years of fighting had maimed many men which, as we have seen, was a reason why the various benevolent bodies, such as the Discharged and Demobilized Soldiers Federation, had been founded. By royal initiative, a national fund was inaugurated, known as the King's Fund, aimed at assisting disabled servicemen to become useful members of society. George V started the ball rolling with an initial donation of £78,000, so when a list was opened in Crewe at a sparsely attended meeting, J.H. Kettell, the Mayor, headed Crewe's subscription list with a cheque for fifty pounds, a not inconsiderable amount. Over the next four weeks it reached the dizzy heights of £253. The idea of a charity to supplement the pension of disabled soldiers must have caused controversy locally, as there were articles in the *Chronicle* justifying the morality of a fund dependent upon the public's generosity when the injuries had been caused in defence of the state.

By late summer the papers were optimistically commenting that the Germans were on the run, with thousands killed and many more surrendering. Lloyd George, the Prime Minister, said on 9 August:

'If anybody had told General Ludendorf on March 22 that up to the month of August he would be trying to get his guns away from the advancing French and British armies ... well I don't know German ... but I believe it would be very strong language.'

From now on the war news would all be mainly positive. Gone, never to return, was the day only four months previously when Dr Wilson was appealing for recruits to fill the vacant ranks of the Crewe Volunteers in case the Germans invaded. As summer turned to autumn it was apparent that the end was near, especially when the *Chronicle* reported in October that the Germans had requested an armistice. At the same time the editor was concerned lest the peace overtures were a guise to keep the Fatherland's borders inviolate, so that they could boast that 'no invader's foot had trodden on the sacred soil of Germany.'

It must not be assumed that this plea for peace was achieved without continuing sacrifice, as a glance at the casualties highlighted in the local papers will reveal. Almost as many Crewe men were killed between July and November 1918 (ninety-two) than the same months in 1916 (ninety-eight) which included the great Somme battle. Fighting was continuing across all the fronts, though it was France that claimed the most victims. August witnessed the death in action of seventeen Crewe men, including Private Fred Saunders (Wistaston Road),

Private Stanley Cornes who was interred near Poperinghe in Belgium, after dying of wounds received during the closing weeks of the war, was remembered on the family's grave marker. Before enlisting into the Cheshires he lived in Bedford Street and worked as an LNWR storekeeper.

who formerly worked in the Steel Works Time Office, in addition to teaching in a Sunday school. Poignantly, he was killed exactly a year after his brother. Another August widow was the wife of Private Charles A. Morgan (Gainsborough Road) of the Coldstream Guards who is buried in Croisilles British Cemetery, leaving a vacancy in the Chief Accountant's Office. Private Samuel Long (Culland Street), who had served in Gallipoli and Egypt with the Cheshires before being transferred to France, was wounded on 20 July when his battalion, attached to the Tenth French Army, counter-attacked against German positions north of Soissons. Five days later he died and became the solitary representative of the Cheshires with a grave in Verberie French National Cemetery.

The last six weeks of the war were the worst for Crewe deaths than any other similar period excepting the July of 1916, so we must therefore include a few details of some who never came back. Lance Corporal William Kellet (Collins Street) of the Manchester Regiment died on 2 November from the effects of gas. The same day saw the death of Second Lieutenant William J. Bowler (Nile Street), son of a Crewe builder, serving with the newly formed RAF. John Clarke (Market Terrace), fighting with the Lancashire Fusiliers, was killed two days later, not far from Wilfred Owen, the poet and a lieutenant with the Manchesters. They both lie in Ors Communal Cemetery.

Deaths on other fronts that autumn were caused as much by disease as bullets and shells. Private Henry Walker, who enlisted out of the North Steam Sheds in 1914, when he was 17, served throughout the war, only to be killed in Salonika in October 1918. Driver Arthur Amson (Meredith Street), of the Crewe Artillery contingent, succumbed to dysentery in Egypt, aged 22, while Driver Leonard Nothard (Lawton Street) of the RGA died one month later of malarial fever in Alexandra Hospital. It was recorded of him that he received a bible when he entered Jerusalem in December 1917.

Awards came thick and fast at this fearsome time, such as the bar to his Military Medal won by Sergeant J.D. Nixon (Ruskin Road), or the Military Medal gained by Private T.C. Shaw (Broad Street), aged 17, having enlisted with the Cheshires aged around 14. All the pupils at the Secondary School must have cheered when it was announced that an ex-student, Lieutenant Duncan Cumming, had won a bar to his Military Cross, as the head gave them a day's holiday in recognition of his achievement. Another officer, W.A. Beckett (Newcastle Street) of the South Lancashire Regiment, was awarded an MC in the July counter-attack, having taken charge when his company commander was killed. Beckett, unusually for an officer, only received an elementary education at West Street Council School. The headmistress there was Miss Parkinson, who herself was mentioned in dispatches for 'her valuable service rendered during the war.' At the commencement of hostilities she had enrolled with the St John's Ambulance and Nursing Services.

On Monday 11 November a few seconds after 11.00 am the LNWR Works buzzer gave a long blast, a sound which signalled the end of the four year struggle. Though the public knew the end was near, there were none of the instant news services that we are so used to today, consequently the end was somewhat abrupt. Thousands thronged the streets, including all the LNWR employees, who had downed tools in a rush to join the general celebrations. Flags were flown from every public building, bunting was slung across streets, Christ Church's bells pealed for many hours and most people wore rosettes decorated with the colours of the Allies. Bands soon assembled, playing patriotic

Ladies from the wartime canteen, organised by the Church of England Men's Society, posing at the railway station. Altogether about 350 women were needed to service the canteen, which never closed. *(Mary and Colin Maclean)*

music, while the crowd sang Rule Britannia and the national anthem. According to the *Chronicle*, young women walked around the streets singing popular songs and hymns, which was much more dignified than copulating in doorways to celebrate the war's end, as claimed by A.J.P. Taylor in his celebrated work, *English History 1914-1945*.

The feelings of the younger generation that Monday were recorded in the *Gridiron*, the magazine of the Secondary School in Ruskin Road:

> 'At the moment when the glad news came through to Crewe and the buzzers began blowing, we were in the midst of the morning interval. The interval was much prolonged, speculation was rife, rumours of every sort were flying about. Little groups of excited people were to be seen … . It seemed impossible to believe that the guns on the battlefields that had boomed out death and destruction … were silent … the terrible and dastardly Hun … was at last beaten.'

This Christmas card was from the 7th Division, which during part of 1916/17 fought in Flanders, where Lance Corporal Herbert Bentley, of Brook Street, was one of three Crewe men killed in action while fighting with the 20th Battalion, Manchester Regiment, part of the Division. *(Mary and Colin Maclean)*

If the war had continued the boy, F.G. who wrote these words would himself have been called to the colours.

Owing to the shortage of ale and spirits, there was very little drunkenness. Despite most schools being closed on account of the flu epidemic, McCurtain, the headmaster, gave a stirring speech at a specially arranged assembly on Tuesday morning, explaining how former pupils had helped to rid the world of German tyranny. Whereas Bowen Cooke, of the LNWR, had promised that Monday would be a paid holiday, he expected all employees to be at their bench on Tuesday. He may as well have saved his breath, as hardly any heeded his call. All the churches had celebratory thanksgiving services, where the collection was usually given to the King's Fund for disabled soldiers. Shades on the street lights were removed which, coupled with the local papers returning to their normal size, were further signs of the war's end. Some streets organized bonfires (a sure sign of an English celebration) on which were burned effigies of the Kaiser. And so it was that Crewe marked the conclusion of the fearsome struggle of the Great War.

Chapter Six

1919 Returning to Normal?

'Every day we live now will bring us back something the red-hand of war snatched from us and, as we go forward with lightened spirits, a new feeling of courage and hope will rise up within us.' *Crewe Guardian* 3 January 1919

JUST BECAUSE AN Armistice had been agreed did not mean that life returned to normal in Crewe, which was suffering from Spanish influenza, a pandemic that was sweeping through Europe. The same week that the killing stopped in France and almost all the other areas of conflict, the cemetery staff in the Broad Street burial ground had their hours extended to cope with all the extra funerals caused by the 'flu epidemic. To combat the flu, it was recommended by the *Chronicle* to always breathe through the nose, sneeze morning and evening, wear nothing tight around the neck and walk home from work. Despite this advice the average number of deaths per month for the first nine months of 1918 was forty, whereas for the last three months it averaged eighty-four, although by April 1919 it had run its course. It is quite a telling statistic that local deaths through the 1918 influenza epidemic, or its corollary, pneumonia, totalled 35 per cent of all the Crewe military fatalities caused by enemy action in the Great War.

Sadly, even soldiers who were alive on 11 November succumbed to 'flu during the ensuing weeks. Lieutenant

Even after the Armistice soldiers died as a consequence of the 'flu epidemic. Private Peter Murphy was one such soldier. Notice, however, from the inscription, how Private Murphy had earlier in the war assisted in blood transfusions and skin grafts.

Great War veterans marching proudly along West Street on their way to the Square for the Remembrance Service in November 1937. In the background can be seen the West Street Baptist Church (formerly Tabernacle).

Charles Booth, who was returning home on HMS *Hazel* after service in the Royal Navy Reserve, died from influenza. His grave is in the East Mudros military cemetery on the Greek island of Lemnos, where he was one of the last Englishmen to be buried. About nine months previously his mother had passed away. The Booth family had lived in Rainow, an eight bedroom property on Nantwich Road, which also boasted large grounds and a tennis court. This house was sold to Pat Collins, the showman, so Charles would

1919 RETURNING TO NORMAL

have had to find another home if he had ever reached England.

The cessation of hostilities meant that demobilized servicemen began to return home to Crewe, though perhaps the greatest civic welcome was reserved for returning prisoners of war, when in March 1919 over a hundred repatriated PoWs were invited to a banquet at the Crewe Arms Hotel. This dinner had been arranged by the LNWR employees committee that had concerned itself with the welfare of prisoners of war for over three years, regularly sending parcels of food or clothes to every incarcerated Crewe man. Its record of care is praise worthy, for between 1915 and 1918 thousands of packages had been despatched at a cost of thousands of pounds. In addition this committee had sponsored two beds in a base hospital in France, along with an annual maintenance donation. It was also supporting St Dunstan's Home for the Blind, the Crewe Red Cross Hospital, and a one off grant of £140 to the Halmer End Pit Disaster of 1918, when 155 men lost their lives.

Also present at the banquet, in the Crewe Arms, were the recently elected Mayor C.J. Bowen Cooke, Sir Gilbert Claughton, chairman of the LNWR and other directors. Local guests included H.S.K. Feltham (Town Clerk), Captain H.P.M. Beames, Major Jackson and Delhi Hughes, the chairman of the committee. This latter man became a well-known dance impresario in Crewe during the inter-war years. One of the PoWs, picked out for a press mention, was Sergeant E. Evans, who escaped from a camp in Germany after working down a coal mine for twelve months. Sir Gilbert took the opportunity in his speech of welcome to warn against the growing strength of the unions in their pursuit of wage rises.

This growth and rising power of organized labour seems to have been a direct result of wartime conditions. The Crewe branch of the National Union of General Workers, which had eighty-six members in 1914, increased to 558 by 1917, partly through the efforts of John Williams, whose name has been mentioned previously. The Railway Clerks' Association had only one local branch in 1914, yet three in 1919, with well over a thousand registered members. In the immediate post-war years this led to disharmony, as the Town Council retained its predominance of shopkeepers and commercial interests. Samuel Jackson, a local industrialist, and a Guardian of the Poor, commenting on a claim for a rise in wages from the Poor Law Workers' Union, said:

> 'The miners had bluffed the government, the railway workers had bluffed the government to the extent of adding 100 million a year to the cost of railway maintenance ... with a debt of eight thousand million the country would go from bad to worse.'

The said union was only asking for a small reduction in hours, a demand that even the *Chronicle* accepted was reasonable.

It cannot be denied that the war years engendered a militant spirit amongst a large proportion of the nation's industrial workers and that was reflected in Crewe. In an Oxford undergraduate dissertation, John Colclough pin-pointed 1916-1920 as a time when the [Crewe Cooperative] Society was politicised and radicalized by a general leftward shift of working-class opinion.' A shift was certainly revealed by the 'Khaki Election' of 1918, when J.T. Brownlie increased the Labour vote from 2,485 to 10,439.

This vehicle, which according to the author of *Light Railways in the First World War*, was rather ineffective, was manufactured in the LNWR Works at Crewe. Just over 130 of these Crewe tractors were made for service on the battlefields.

In the local election one month later the Labour Party achieved a clean sweep of all available seats.

In his book *Deeds of a Great Railway*, George Darroch records the contribution to the national effort made by the LNWR works in Crewe, a contribution that can only be outlined here. A hybrid vehicle that travelled along roads, or rails, with the minimum of conversion, known as the Crewe tractor, was fashioned in the works, along with armoured trains, howitzer guns of various sizes, quick-firing guns, anti-aircraft guns, gun carriages, limbers for gun carriages and waggons, graze fuses and cable-wire. In this context, Darroch includes a list of the many and varied parts that were needed to complete this material of war, all manufactured at Crewe. He also emphasized the crucial contribution of the women workers. Add to this its strategic position on the railway system, with countless traffic movements over the four years of war, and some indication of the importance of Crewe is clear to see.

One aspect of calling young men to a life in the trenches that was rarely openly mentioned in the war years was the drive for sex. Most of the recruits went to battle encouraged by the words of the local parson or minister of religion to 'keep clean and act like a man'. No doubt the majority did, yet it has been suggested with some justification that a soldier was more likely to be admitted to hospital with venereal disease (VD), than with trench foot. Siegfried Sassoon in his poem '*They*' makes reference to this:

Poor Jim's shot through the lungs and like to die;
And Bert's gone syphilitic;

According to Mark Harrison, over sixty thousand men serving in France were treated in hospitals for VD in 1918, which is a rate of just over thirty-two men per thousand troops. Other authorities put the figure of infection at around 5 per cent of all service personnel. If this percentage is extrapolated to Crewe, it would suggest that well over two hundred men caught VD while serving in the forces. This subject has been mentioned because the Medical Officer of Health's (MOH) report for 1919 bemoans the absence of a facility locally for treating VD:

'That such is required is clearly indicated by the increase in the number of new born infants …suffering from ophthalmia neonatorum.'

This was caused by the mother being infected with either gonorrhoea or chlamydia, another not so well reported consequence of the war.

The MOH's report also made mention of the dearth of housing in Crewe, which had also been featured in a Local Government Report of 1918, where it was estimated that over 600 houses were needed to meet the current demand. One answer from the Town Council was to appoint a sub-committee in January 1919 to look into the problem. The only major building projects during the war years were the Co-operative Society's Bakery and the Prudential Buildings, with no house plans being passed after April 1916. The first practical step to meet the acute housing shortage was taken by the Mayor, Bowen Cooke, when he arranged for fifty ex-army huts to be erected in Victoria Avenue. In October 1919, the deliberations of the council's sub-committee began to bear fruit, when Sir Gilbert Claughton ceremonially cut the first sod of the Claughton Avenue estate, meaning that the shortage caused by war-time conditions was being partially rectified.

Another factor that impinged upon the housing crisis was an increase in the number of babies born in the town when the troops returned. The birth rate had declined from an average of 31.8 between the years 1900 and 1904, to 18.07 in the five years after 1914. By 1920 it was back to 21.05, though it must be stated, however, that the effect of an increased birth rate should not be exaggerated, as it had been declining for a number of years owing to young men leaving Crewe to seek employment elsewhere, as the town's economy was unable to support them.

Cessation of hostilities also meant that the war-time charities were wound up. April saw the closure of the Red Cross Hospital in Webb's Orphanage, in addition to the St John's Hospital in France, where Mary Warneford had acted as a superintendent and the LNWR Committee had contributed towards its upkeep. Crewe's League of Friendliness, with its membership of 2,000, held its last meeting in March. The War Canteen on the station turned off its taps and bade farewell to its 400 voluntary workers. In December the committee of the Sailors' and Soldiers' Rest on Nantwich Road held a final meeting to disperse the surplus balance of £1,200. Since 1915 it was estimated that one and a half million servicemen had used its facilities. The Dale Tobacco Fund, that had provided smokes for the troops, was closed down before the end of 1918.

Peace Day was celebrated on 19 July by decorating the streets, playgrounds, Square and the Park. Bands played around the streets where people, horses and dogs sported patriotic ribbons. All the Councillors and officials gathered on the square for a service, before removing to the park, where the greatest gathering in its history had assembled. Ten thousand children were entertained with races and sports, while adults swam in the lake, watched a variety show, or witnessed the planting of memorial oaks brought from Verdun. Mention was made in the speeches of the death of Captain Walter Warneford, who only a few weeks earlier had piloted his airship NS11 over Crewe, where he had served his apprenticeship. The only negative notes reported were that some Crewe servicemen were still overseas, and also the town was celebrating peace without involving the men maimed and disabled by the war.

A visit, by Sir Arthur Conan Doyle in June 1919, to lecture on 'Death and the After Life' in the Town Hall, presided over by Bowen Cooke, is symptomatic of a religious sentiment that was felt in all parts of the nation. Owing to so many families losing members there was a passionate desire to contact them, leading to a growing interest in spiritualism, hoping that thereby they could contact their loved one 'on the other side'. A few weeks later the *Chronicle* reported that Conan Doyle had been photographed at Crewe surrounded by spirits. As it happened, the town became quite well-known nationally as the home of the Crewe Circle, a group of psychical photographers, led by William Hope from his premises on Nantwich Road.

Arthur Ryder, who lived in Chambers Street, recorded the following incident in his unpublished memoirs:

> 'Mrs Wild ... was a real character ... She was a spiritualist and her husband had died in the first world war. She came across one morning and told us that her husband had knocked on the bedroom window telling her to turn her bed around the other way because he could not see her. Dad went across to help her do it.'

Whether or not Mrs Wild ever made contact with her dead husband, it is certain the

A Great War tank was given to Crewe in recognition of the town's contribution to war savings. This image, from 1926, shows Frank Kettell (Ruskin Road) in Queens Park with a group of children from his Sunday school in Underwood Lane.

Crewe Spiritualist Society had sufficient members by the end of 1920 to rent a hut near Mill Street Bridge and to begin regular services.

In June the War Trophies Committee offered Crewe a German machine gun, an ammunition belt and box, all of which Alderman Jervis claimed were worthless, and that Germany should keep her old stuff. What did prove acceptable was the tank, handed over in October, as a token acknowledgement of the large sum collected and invested in war savings. At a reception service on the Square, onlookers were charged a small fee to look around it. This war relic was later displayed in the Park, where it stayed until about 1928. Many of the workshops in the LNWR works erected their own memorials to the fallen, as did some of the other employers, such as the Crewe Co-operative Society and the Post Office.

Even before the end of the conflict, schemes to mark in a suitable way the sacrifice of so many Crewe men were being mentioned in the Council Chamber and the local press. Amongst these schemes was a vehicular bridge

One suggested scheme to commemorate the war was to build a row of alms type houses in Victoria Avenue. This is an artist's impression of how they could have appeared if the project had gone ahead. *(Adrian Smith)*

Another suggestion for a Memorial was to create and landscape a walk along the Valley Brook from Walthall Street to the Park. *(Adrian Smith)*

across the Valley Brook in Flag Lane, public baths, concert hall, extension to Queen's Park, paved walk-way along the brook to the Park, or memorial houses in Victoria Avenue. All were considered, but rejected for one reason or another. For instance the walk-way scheme would have entailed 12,000 cubic yards of excavation, 43,000 yards of earth for artificial banks and construction of a dam and bridges. In March the *Chronicle*'s comment was:

'People do not want a Memorial on the Market Square as that would be useless as well as a bit of a nuisance and a complete waste of money.'

Despite this negative remark, the town did have a statue on the Square, which was unveiled in June 1924 by Sir Ian Hamilton of Gallipoli fame. By this date, the town had settled once more into the rhythms of normal life that was to be interrupted from time to time by the General Strike and the financial depression of the thirties. Sadly, the words of Sir Ian Hamilton came true, and the politicians, along with most of the

United Methodist Church,
HIGHTOWN, CREWE.

Sunday Afternoon, January 15th,
1922, at 2-30.

Service of Dedication
of
Memorial Window

TO THE MEN OF HIGHTOWN CHURCH & SCHOOL WHO, IN THE GREAT WAR OF 1914-19,
——— MADE ———
"The Supreme Sacrifice."

REV. ERNEST SHEPPARD
will conduct the Service, and
SIR WILLIAM HODGSON
will unveil the Window.

Order of Service for the dedication of a Memorial Window at the United Free Methodist (later Heathfield) church. Sir William Hodgson, a Baptist, was knighted for services to education in Cheshire. He lived in Helmsville, about a hundred yards from the church, the only knight ever to dwell in the confines of Crewe.

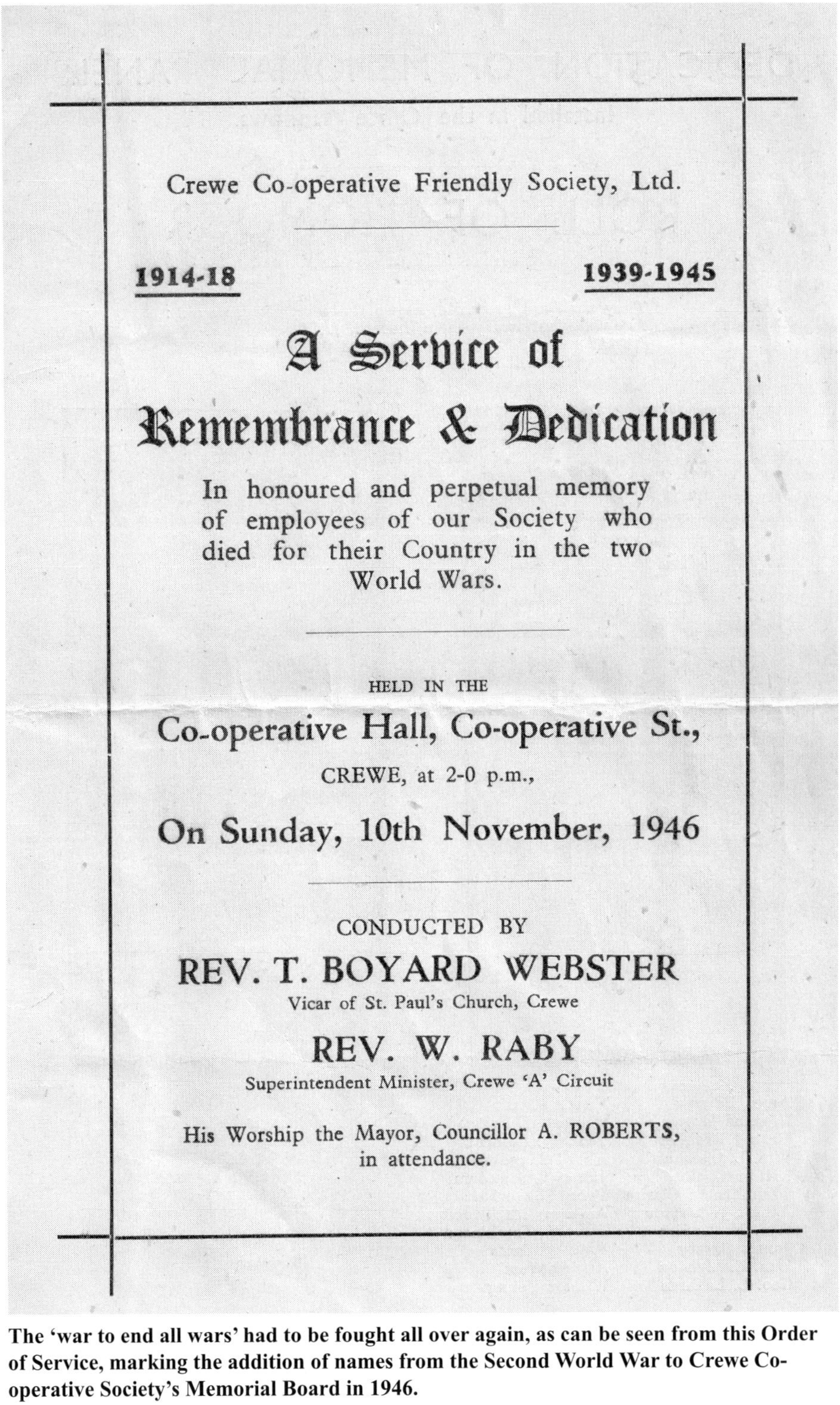

Crewe Co-operative Friendly Society, Ltd.

1914-18 **1939-1945**

A Service of Remembrance & Dedication

In honoured and perpetual memory of employees of our Society who died for their Country in the two World Wars.

HELD IN THE

Co-operative Hall, Co-operative St.,

CREWE, at 2-0 p.m.,

On Sunday, 10th November, 1946

CONDUCTED BY

REV. T. BOYARD WEBSTER
Vicar of St. Paul's Church, Crewe

REV. W. RABY
Superintendent Minister, Crewe 'A' Circuit

His Worship the Mayor, Councillor A. ROBERTS, in attendance.

The 'war to end all wars' had to be fought all over again, as can be seen from this Order of Service, marking the addition of names from the Second World War to Crewe Co-operative Society's Memorial Board in 1946.

The War Memorial on Crewe Square was made from bronze and modelled on Britannia. On 14 June 1924 it was unveiled by General Sir Ian Hamilton and the Bishop of Chester in the presence of the Mayor, John Jackson, and a large crowd, to commemorate all of the men from Crewe who fell in the Great War.

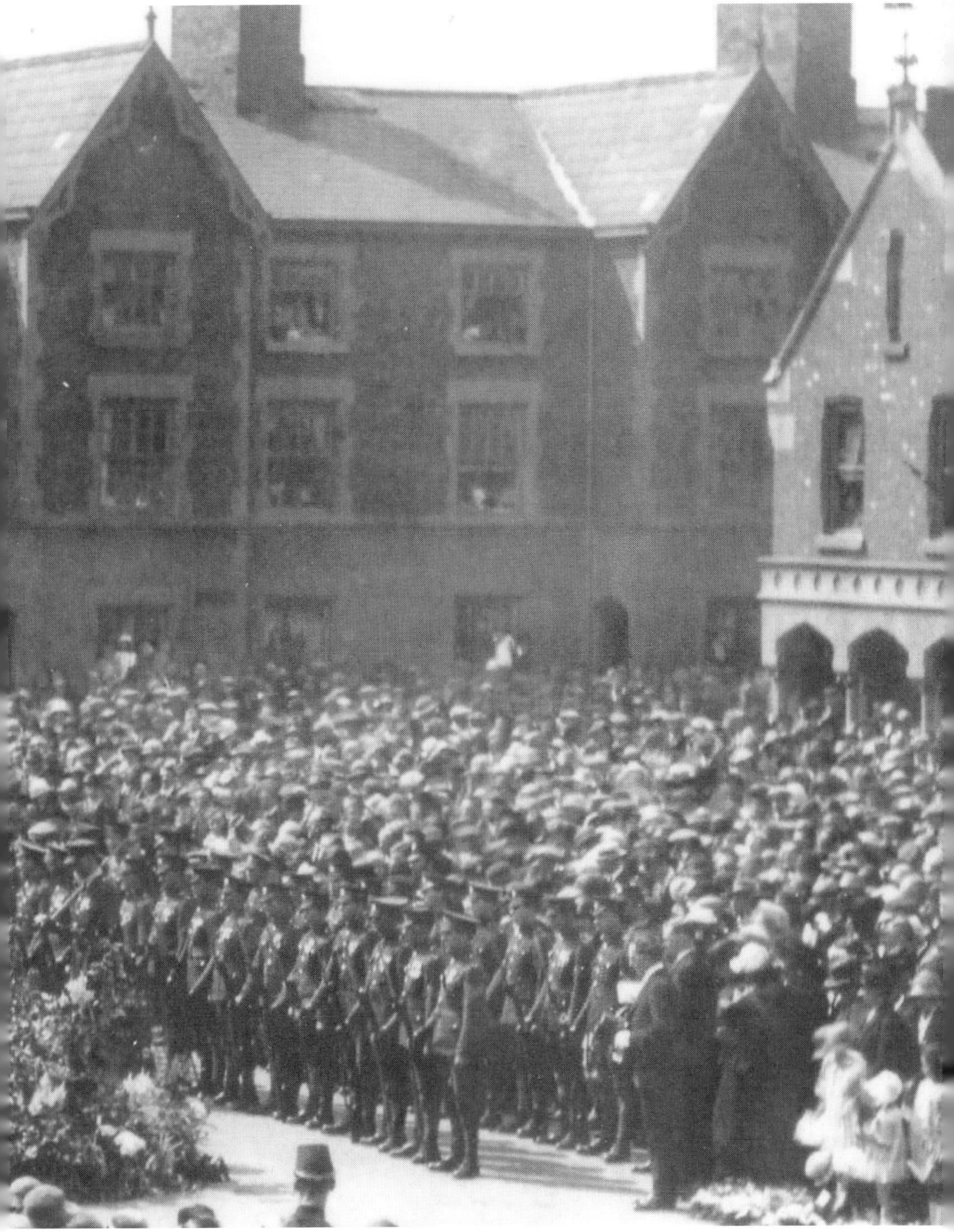

population, drifted into another armed conflict with the same principal enemy. Nothing is learned from history.

As we have reached the end of this book on Crewe and the Great War, it would only be right for the last word to be given by one who was there. Gunner Joseph Knight, a local man, recorded this last entry in his wartime diary:

> 'Arrived Plymouth Sound and Harbour. Night of the 25 went to Prees Heath demob centre. Arrived there morning of Friday, settle up and away again by night time. I arrived home Friday night 26 September 1919.'

Gunner Knight was one of the lucky ones who returned home able to pick up the threads of his life once more. Or was he lucky? Was anyone lucky that went through such a conflict, even if they came home physically unscarred? I think not!

BIBLIOGRAPHY

Source: Crewe Public Library & Cheshire Record Office
Census Enumerator's Report 1891: 1901: 1911:
Crewe Chronicle
Crewe Guardian
Crewe Sailors & Soldiers Rest Visitors' Book
Minutes of Council & Committee Meetings (1910-1925) Crewe Town Council
The Times

Unpublished Dissertations, Memoirs & Articles
Anon	Diary of Service in Mesopotamia with the RASC January-August 1918
Colclough, J.	The Co-operative Friendly Society 1900/1921 the Politics of Class and Consumption in a Northern Railway Town (2010)
Harrison, M.	The British Army & the Problem of Venereal Disease Medical History (1995)
Hodgkison, W.W.	Telling it Like it Was (1969)
Howes, G.	Memories of Forty-nine Years' Service with the LNWR (1940)
Knight, Gunner J.	Diary of Service in Mesopotamia with the Machine Gun Corps
Ryder, D.A.	Dabbers and Creweites

Printed Books
Anon.	*Zeppeline uber England* (1916)
Chaloner, W.H.	*The Social & Economic Development of Crewe* (1950)
Clayton, A.	*Chavasse Double VC* (2006)
Crookenden, A.	*The History of the Cheshire Regiment in the Great War*
Cooper, W.	*From Early Life* (1990)
Darroch, G.	*Deeds of a Great Railway* (1920)
Eardley, W.	*Crewe Almanack* (various dates)
Holmes, R.	*Acts of War* (2004)
Holmes, R.	*Tommy* (2004)
Lear, W.	*Down the Rabbit Hole* (1975)
Liddell Hart, B.	*History of the First World War* (1992 reprint)
MacDonald, L	*The Last Man, Spring 1918* (1998)
Middlebrook, M.	*The First Day on the Somme* (1971)
Middlebrook, M.	*The Kaiser's Battle* (1978)
Middlebrook, M.	*The Somme Battlefields* (1994)
Potts & Marks	*Crewe & Nantwich at War* (2007) 2 vols
Stallworthy, J.	*Wilfred Owen a biography* (1974)
Taylor, A.J.P.	*English History 1914-1945* (1963)
Wilson, J.M.	*Siegfried Sassoon* (1998)

Monumental Masonry
Crewe War Memorial
Graves in Crewe Cemetery
LNWR Tranship Shed War Memorial

Web Sites
1914-1918 Long, Long Trail
Commonwealth War Graves Commission
War Service Records

Index

Abortion, 61
Allotments, 55
Amson, Driver A., 78
Ankers, Pte N., 60
Asquith, H.H., 28, 31, 49, 52
Asquith, Lt R., 49
Atkinson, Dr J., 60,
Austin, L/Cpl J., 59

Bailey, Dr E., 15
Barrow, Pte A., 34
Barrow, Sgt W., 26
Basra War Memorial, 57, 60, 73
Bates, C., 26
Battle of:
    Aisne, 18, 47
    Cambrai, 70
    Dardanelles, 37
    Dogger Bank, 35
    Gallipoli, 30, 78, 88
    Gaza, 70
    Jutland, 35, 45–6
    Kaiser's, 72
    La Basee, 18, 47
    Loos, 38, 47, 64
    Marne, 18, 47
    Mons, 18, 24, 41, 47
    Neuve Chapelle, 30, 34
    Somme, 20, 31, 46, 48–50, 56–7, 63–4, 70, 77
    Ypres, 18, 34–6 43, 47, 53, 63–4
Beames, Capt, H.P., 64, 83
Bebbington, Sgt T., 34
Beckett, 2/Lt W.A., 78
Belgian Refugees, 17, 32
Berks, Pte R., 31
Bidlake, Rev W.A., 14, 26, 46, 76
Birkenhead, 35, 51
Birth Rate, 86
Black-out, 33, 43
Booth, C., 82
Bostock, 2/Lt J., 86
Bottomley, H., 50
Bowler, 2/Lt W.J., 78
Boy Scouts, 36, 51, 73
Bradley, A., 35, 45
Britannia Brick Company, 62
British Legion, 74

Broadhurst, Sgt J., 53
Broughton, Pte W., 46
Brown, Pte T., 52
Bullock, Clr H., 57
Burnell, J., 13, 34

Cannon, Pte W., 54
Cartwright, Pte A., 48
Cartwright, Sgt J., 57
Charnock, G., 74–6
Charnock, S., 45
Chavasse, Capt N., 49, 36
Christmas Truce, 21–2, 40
Churchill, W.S., 67
Claughton, Sir G., 83, 85
Clayton, Pte T., 49–50
Clynes, J.R., 60
Colclough, J., 84
Colclough, Sapper L.G., 60
Coleman, Pte W., 64
Collins, P., 75, 82
Conde, Pte N., 70
Cooke, Bowen C.J., 16, 24, 30–2, 36, 51, 61, 80, 83, 85
Cooke, Pte F., 24
Cooke, Miss M., 36
Cost of Living, 12, 25, 60
Crabtree, Pte W., 56
Craig, Sir E., 16–17, 23, 30–1, 36, 51, 61
Crewe Artillery Battery, 14–15, 19, 60, 64–5, 78
Crewe Brotherhood, 67, 76
Crewe Co-operative Society, 12–13, 48–9, 60, 69, 71–2, 85
Crewe Irish League, 46
Crewe Primrose League, 17
Crewe Sailors and Soldiers Families Association, 17
Cumming, 2/Lt G., 49
Cumming, Lt D., 78

Dale Tobacco Fund, 17, 43, 86
Darroch, G., 76, 85
Davenport, Pte G., 18
Davies, J., 29, 31, 54, 61
Daylight Saving, 44
Dean, Pte A.H., 72
Dean, Pte F., 49
Defence of the Realm Act, 42, 61, 69

INDEX

Dentith, Cpl R., 72
Derby Scheme, 31, 40
Discharged Soldiers & Sailors Association, 74
Dishart, W., 32
Dodd, Pte D., 13
Dodd, Sister E., 39, 59
Dodd, Capt G., 71
Doyle, Sir A., Conan, 86
Dudley, Pte T., 57
Dunn, Sgt S.L., 63
Dunne, Pte J., 34
Dutton, Pte R., 70
Dutton, Guardsman, T., 49

Eardley, W., 11, 35, 38, 44, 57
Eaton, Pte W.H., 60
Eaton-Shore, Lt J.J., 52
Edge, Gunner W., 57–8
Edwards, Pte J., 70
Evans, Sgt E., 83
Evans, Pte L., 70
Evans, Pte T.C., 48

Farrell, Pte E., 24, 54
Farrington, CSM H., 58, 72
Feltham, HSK, 14, 29, 68, 83
Fincken, C., 46
Flude, T., 62
Francis, Sapper F., 37

Gill, J., 18
Gladden, Gunner W., 65
Graves, R., 49
Groby Farm, 55

Harrison, Pte A., 48
Harrop, A., 15
Hayes, Sgt A.G., 18
Heeson, Pte J., 54
Hinde, Pte J., 53
Hodgkison, E., 29, 37, 43
Hodkinson, Cpl R., 64
Holdaway, R., 55
Holdcroft, Pte H., 55
Holme, Sapper J., 34
Home Defence Volunteers, 31–2, 36, 51, 76–7
Hoptroff, H., 60
Housing, 70, 85–6
Hughes, D., 83
Hulme, Pte P., 38

Ineson, B.G., 45
Influenza, 81–2
Irish Rebellion, 46

Jackson, Maj J.N., 32, 36, 83, 90
Jervis, Clr. A., 28, 32, 87
Jones, Sgt A., 14
Jones, Pte A., 21–2
Jones, Cpl F.A., 24, 34
Jones, Lt L., 45

Kellett, L/Cpl W., 78
Kettell, Alderman, J.H., 27, 42, 45, 50, 54, 77
King, Pte A.C., 18
King's Fund, 77, 90
Kinlay, A., 13, 24
Kinnick, Pte J., 45
Kitchener, Earl, 15–17, 28–9, 72
Knight, Gunner J., 92

Labour Party, 11–12, 50, 61, 84–5
League of Friendliness, 17, 26, 34, 86
Lewis, R.S., 43
Liberal Party, 27–8, 65
Lightfoot, Pte R., 43
Lightfoot, Lt W., 35
Linnell, CSM J., 59–60
Liquor Trade, 69–70
Livingstone, Gunner P., 35
Lloyd George, D., 8, 30, 36, 52, 60, 73, 77
LNWR Employees' Committee, 26, 53, 74, 78, 83
Lockett, Pte A., 72
Long, Pte S., 78
Lowe, G., 33
Lupton, Pte A., 72
Lusitania, RMS, 36, 59
Lyon, Lt C., 59
Lyon, Sister E., 59

Maddock, Pte J.W., 56
Malam, Cpl F., 60
Manley, E.H., auctioneer, 36, 52
Manley, Pte H., 18
Marriott, Pte T., 63
McCurtain, D.H., 36, 80
McNeill, Alderman W., 27–8, 36, 65
Measles, 38
Menin Gate Memorial, 36, 62, 64
Military Service Act, 40, 45

Mills, Sgt J.E., 37
Moorhouse, S., 45
Morgan, Pte C.A., 78
Mullock, Pte W., 34

Nantwich, 7, 17, 21, 32, 41, 68
Nat Fed Discharged Soldiers and Sailors, 70, 74
Nat Union of General Workers, 60, 83
Nat Union of Railwaymen, 11, 40
National Registration Act, 31
National War Aims, 61, 67
Nicol, Pte W., 36
Nield, Pte A., 57
Nield, Pte C., 48
Nixon, E., 15
Nixon, Sgt J.D., 78
Nothard, Driver L., 78

Oldham, Sgt F.H., 15

Palestine, 47, 65, 74
Palin, Pte T.H., 27, 40
Parkinson, Miss E., 78
Parsons, L/Sgt G., 43
Paul, Pte A., 18
Pearson, 2/Lt G., 65
Pettigrew, Pte J., 24
Prisoners of War, 15, 23–6, 35, 40, 43, 53–4, 70, 83
Prophett, Pte H., 35
Proudlove, Gunner S., 59

Ranicar, Pte J.W., 72
Red Cross, 37, 41, 52–4, 56–9, 67, 83, 86
Reeves, Pte J.G., 45
Riley, Pte A., 49
Rimmer, Pte J.R., 31
Riots, 19–20
Rogerson, Pte J., 45
Ryder, A., 86

Sassoon, S., 49, 61, 85
Saunders, Pte F., 77
Shaw, Pte T.C., 78
Sherwin, Gunner, 24
Smith, Pte W., 65
Snelson, Miss D., 59
Sparrow, Cpl G.W., 47
Spiritualism, 86

St John's Ambulance Brigade, 15, 54, 58, 78, 86
Stelfox, Pte C., 51
Strawport, Pte N., 72
Struthers, 2/Lt W., 72
Stubbs, Gunner A., 72

Tench, Rifleman W., 43
Thiepval Memorial, 50
Tipping, 2/Lt F.B., 64
Titanic, RMS, 71
Tomkinson, Rifleman W., 70

Urquhart, W., 43–4

Vaughan, Clr E., 14
Vaughan, Bombardier W., 53
Venables Sapper A., 71
Venereal Disease, 85
Vickers, C., 38
Villiers Russell twins, 13, 24, 48, 72

Walker, Pte H., 78
Walker, W., 45
Wallis, Clr G., 72
Walters, Pte H., 71
Walters, J., 45
Ward Brothers, 15, 38
Warneford, Mrs M., 17, 58, 86
Warneford, W., 46, 86
Warneford, W.H.H., 46
Welch, Lt W., 14–15, 65, 70
Wilkinson, G., 41
Williams, Clr J., 12, 16, 29–30, 50, 60, 84
Williams, Pte J., 18
Williams, Rifleman J.B., 53
Williamson, Pte J., 39
Wilson, Dr C., 20, 77
Withoff, Clr F.W., 20, 32, 62
Wolbrom, Pte T., 71
Women's Employment, 30–3, 38, 63, 73, 76, 85
Women's Imperial Defence Council, 50
Woodhouse, 2/Lt G.F., 49

Yardley, Pte J., 48
Yates, Clr E., 25, 50

Zeppelin Airships, 33–4, 41–2, 46–7, 57, 67